Business Ethics and Rational Corporate Policies

Business Ethics and Rational Corporate Policies

Leveraging Human Resources in Organizations

Konstantinos Mantzaris

BEP
BUSINESS EXPERT PRESS
Leader in applied, concise business books

Business Ethics and Rational Corporate Policies: Leveraging Human Resources in Organizations

Copyright © Business Expert Press, LLC, 2021.

First published in 2021 by
Business Expert Press, LLC
222 East 46th Street, New York, NY 10017
www.businessexpertpress.com

ISBN-13: 978-1-95253-874-2 (paperback)
ISBN-13: 978-1-95253-875-9 (e-book)

Business Expert Press Business Ethics and Corporate
Citizenship Collection

Collection ISSN: 2333-8806 (print)
Collection ISSN: 2333-8814 (electronic)

Cover and interior design by S4Carlisle Publishing Services Private Ltd.,
Chennai, India

First edition: 2021

10 9 8 7 6 5 4 3 2 1

Printed in the United States of America.

Abstract

Business ethics is a multidimensional field of applied ethics that examines the ethical policies, principles, and moral challenges arising in and through the operations of organizations. Human behavior presents vigorous internal driving forces regarding a personal code of conduct; hence, moral awareness can be quite different among individuals. This book focuses on practices and the development of moral thinking in the context of corporate policy making. It describes moral reasoning by demonstrating the *moral entity consideration* principle. It is vital to understand the human thinking process as a medium to exploit available resources and develop ethical and rational policies to achieve corporate efficiency.

Considering the responsibility of human resources to incorporate business ethics into organizational practice, individual behavior is the key element to create a valuable business culture of fairness, meritocracy, transparency, and trust. The content of the book emphasizes on developing moral and rational thinking skills for corporate governance, and therefore an ethical thinking attitude. It examines how to ethically deal with the demanding corporate policies and procedures, providing a timeless comprehensive guide on how to leverage human resources in organizations and retain a moral identity through rational behavior.

This book is perfect for executives and practitioners in the business ethics field, as well as for scholars and advanced business students who want to enter the corporate world, aiming to develop their mindset capacity of ethical thinking by analyzing the moral aspects of each challenge posed.

Keywords

business ethics; corporate policies; rational policies; human resources; HRM; moral entity consideration; moral thinking, ethical behavior; human behavior; leadership; management; organizational culture; ethical information systems; employment relations

Contents

To those who have a positive and vital impact on my everyday communication and experience

Preface

This book is the result of an intensive effort to contribute to the highly demanding and multilayered field of business ethics. It attempts to provide the reader with an opportunity to develop the critical principle of *moral entity consideration.* The aim is to understand, from a moral standpoint and through a behavioral thinking analysis, the ethical dimension of various business procedures, such as policy making, organizational development, leadership and management, business culture, and people management. These operations consist of a continuous challenge for each executive and business ethics practitioner as well as for scholars and advanced business students who want to enter the corporate world.

Developing the capacity of ethical thinking by analyzing the moral aspects of human behavior and corporate procedures is not an easy task, as decision makers have a key role in the sustainability of a business, while their moral mindset is vital for the organizational development. Indeed, it is not feasible to implement business ethics into daily work routine by trying to recall a set of common rules and practices; thus, it is important to develop a moral thinking attitude, which can lead to efficiency in terms of coping with both demanding and unprecedented challenges and dilemmas. Consequently, the purpose of this book is to outline a set of concepts concerning a plethora of corporate challenges with reference to ethical terms and practices. It provides analysis on how to ensure that the needs and requirements of both business ethics and human resources are satisfied without harming other entities of the internal or external environment of a corporation, while it examines how it is feasible to attain moral profit maximization through ethical resource exploitation.

Given that the characteristics of agents are associated with the morality of the business as an entity, corporate policies can be modified and evaluated as ethical or unethical. A corporation cannot act itself, as a legal entity, even if it is capable of exploiting automation implementation. Hence, the quality of people following the decisions is responsible for applying business ethics. As businesspeople claim, doing things right is not the same as doing the right things, and considering that we must not act against the rights of other entities, morality can be achieved without additional force only if we think about how behaviors and ethics can be discovered and analyzed on rather different organizational procedures and practices. Thus, at the end of reading this book, you will be able to efficiently develop a variety of ethical thoughts generated internally by your own enhanced code of conduct. This process is vital in terms of coping with corporate challenges and organizational development in a competitive environment. And remember, if you want to understand business ethics at a deeper and rational level, focus on people's shadows.

Konstantinos Mantzaris
October 2020

Acknowledgments

It is essential to mention that I will always be thankful to the publisher *Business Expert Press* for the opportunity to publish my first ever book, and the great people that I have had the chance to work with during the preparation of the book through publishing. I am grateful for the whole experience, since when I received the book proposal from *BEP*'s contractor at Milton Keynes (near London) Nigel Wyatt to be an international author, then working with the *Business Expert Press* team at New York, primarily with Rob Zwettler, the editor of my book David Wasieleski, as well as Charlene Kronstedt, and finally the team at *S4Carlisle Publishing Services* for the various production stages of the book.

I also wish to express my acknowledgment of support to those individuals who have a positive and vital impact on my everyday communication and experience. It is essential to dedicate your life to something important that will last longer than your life itself. Pondering this, be passionate, rational, moral, and optimize the creative and positive part of your thoughts and interactions with life and other entities. Thank you.

Konstantinos Mantzaris

PART I

Business Ethics and Human Resources

Business ethics is a multidimensional field that most of us can instinctively understand. It is hard to be precisely defined as ethics reflects the norms and developments of each historical period. Given the subjectivity of the decision-making process, depending on the limitations of a unique individual (Ravitch 1989), the latter tend to put aside the ethical conduct under the pressure of nonstabilized environments unless an individual's moral attitude is strong enough to avoid such dilemmas. In addition, the American Nobelist and economist Milton Friedman claimed that the only entities who can have responsibilities are people, not the businesses (Friedman 2007). Thus, considering that the corporation outcome is the result of individuals' decisions on each aspect of its operations, we could conclude that business ethics cannot be applied when the conditions are not clear enough in the context of creating and developing a moral business culture.

The aim of this book is to introduce the reader to a demanding mindset world, where the individual must automatically think about ethics before the final behavior, without the need to remember the rules of moral conduct. Ethical thinking is different among individuals. Considering the repercussion of our practices to other entities is critical for both our career and the organization we work for. The content of this book is about exploring business ethics on a series of corporate procedures and challenges regarding human resources, organizational development, individual well-being, and employment relations. As a reader of *Business Ethics and Rational Corporate Policies*, you have automatic access to a range of concepts and moral thinking development schemes designed to enhance your ethical skills at a wide spectrum of moral awareness. This book gives practitioners such as policy makers, agents, managers and corporate leaders, public administrators, negotiators, and generally experts such as policy and education analysts, the essential tools to implement rational corporate policies under the dynamic pressure of business ethics. Additionally, academicians, scholars, and learners such as academic business students can develop their moral mindset capacity by reading this book as it contributes to the moral thinking process of human behavior at both practical and theoretical levels.

CHAPTER 1

Business Ethics and Rational Policies

Business ethics is a fertile field for philosophical investigation with many dimensions as a result of systematic evaluation of norms and values. Ethics and moral policies are solid instruments that can enhance the survival of a corporation or lead to its failure. It is argued that the failure in ethical leadership has been because of the preoccupation with self and humanistic thinking on autonomy (Knights and O'Learyn 2005). At the same time, it is suggested that many managers are poorly prepared to deal with success, and that a strategic direction is never "set" (Ludwig and Longenecker 1993). Hence, answering whether an action or policy is fair enough for each affected entity, thus moral-ready to be established, is not only critical but also extremely valuable for the status of the corporation and the people behind the legal entity as the most crucial cell in each organization. At this point, it is important to mention that the terms of morals and ethics are considered equivalent and will be used interchangeably, as morals are concerned with the principles of right and wrong behavior, and ethics is moral principles that govern an individual's behavior or the conduct of activity.

Ethics is a branch of philosophy that has been developing for at least 2,500 years, since the time of Socrates, Plato, and Aristotle when their theories advanced to provide a set of principles of human conduct (Brickley, Smith, and Zimmerman 2000). The evolution of business ethics has been very similar to the evolution of social ethics (Lee 1926). We do not have an international agreement on one definition about the subject of business ethics as different social groups, such as philosophers, political scientists, business academics, corporate agents, and trainers, have rather different points of view, due to the subjectivity of ethics. The eighteenth-century philosopher and author of the *Wealth of Nations*, Adam Smith (1723 to 1790), drew attention to the fact that efficient economic transactions frequently rely on self-interested or profit-oriented motives (Borchert 2006). In his view, profit seeking and self-interested activity in business is common, as the "invisible hand" and free market operations lead to the inevitable corporate interest that is against the common good. Additionally, Keynes (2009) stated that the moral problem is concerned with the love of money, as the money motive equals to nine-tenths of the activities of life, while the German philosopher Immanuel Kant (1724 to 1804) focused on the power and limits of human reason as a powerful source for cognition and deliberation.

For the purpose of this book, we could conclude that business ethics relies on individual behavior in the context of norms, values, moral principles, and the endogenous code of conduct. Individuals make decisions endlessly on how to behave as each choice can be conceptualized as an action with concrete approaches and perceptions before, during, and after the action in the form of consequences. Hence, business ethics involves examining appropriate restrictions on the pursuit of interest where the actions of individuals and corporate policies affect other entities by generating conflicting values. Ethics also reflects the culture of an organization, thus achieving a sustainable level of morality that is critical for the rational implementation of corporate policies. Violating common moral rules is not the way to achieve corporate goals. Instead, corporate policies should be rational and consider the entities that will be affected by them.

Consequently, Jones (1991) claimed that ethical decisions must be both legal and morally acceptable to the larger community, while unethical decisions are either illegal or morally unacceptable. However, this definition on ethical judgment of a decision can be challenged by the fact that ethical practices are not always legal, while unethical practices are not illegal necessarily. Agents and corporations as legal entities have the right to act in a variety of methods, and sooner or later, they must cope with legal but unethical, and ethical but illegal dilemmas.

For instance, during a financial crisis or an urgent situation such as a pandemic outbreak followed by a market lockdown, a corporation may need to reduce its workforce in an attempt to increase its profit ratio and therefore retain its sustainable position or to decrease its costs regarding its resources. Layoffs, following all the required procedures by local and international law, are legal in terms of contract rules. But, are they ethical as well? Indeed, we cannot change the legal part for our interest, at least in the context of ethical corporate practices, but leading an employee to unemployment for unreasonable profitability reasons violates an aspect of business ethics and the code of conduct. However, at the same time, the agent can defend this position by mentioning that if the corporation does not reduce its workforce, then the whole company will be at a high risk, which can lead to bankruptcy and serious negative impact for both the corporation and employees. Additionally, pay cuts are not a useful alternative to layoffs because workforce reduction harms the morale less than pay cuts, while the monetary worth of the latter practice is not enough to retain many employees (Bewley 1998).

Moreover, this is the reason why business ethics is a field of so many conflicts between individuals and their perceptions. The ethical issues faced are of an unprecedented scale in terms of the range of their implications within corporate policies and practices. We have learned from corporate history that we cannot manage such complex and systemic issues through ad hoc interventions. We cannot use principles and ignore current challenges. We must recognize that business ethics is not a temporary task and that we must always behave considering morals in order to indicate where, when, and how to intervene.

Indeed, the corporate world and economy in general consist of individuals and entities that each one has its own moral principles, goals, and interests. In this regard, new approaches, thoughts, and trends toward equilibrium alleviate the need for rationality of individual agents, maximization of resource utility, and moral behavior. Implementation of the past or current ethical business models is not always acceptable as practitioners must develop their mindset capacity for *moral entity consideration* and adapt to change. This implies that the extension of the existing models and the application of new moral concepts have the potential to bring new insights on how to leverage the human factor, while the corporate culture is associated with moral principles aligned to both internal norms and social beliefs.

Corporate governance as a set of principles, policies, laws, and decisions is responsible for integrating its own customs to employees from the highest to the lowest levels. Building a governance system that enhances business ethics is one of the most important and demanding challenge. The corporate governance system is crucial for an organization and it is almost as important as its primary business plan. When executed effectively, it can prevent corporate failure, scandals, fraud, and in general retain or develop the corporation in a sustainable way. A business without an effective system of corporate governance cannot succeed in the prism of increased internationalized corporate competitiveness.

It is important to mention that there are three strategic types of organizations: (1) defenders (organizations operate in a more stable and predictable environment), (2) analyzers (organizations operate in both stable environments and markets where new products constantly required), and (3) prospectors (organizations operate in unpredictable environments), followed by a fourth called reactors (organizations operate in an environment of inconsistencies among its strategy, technology, structure, and process) as a form of strategic failure (Miles et al. 1978). Policy makers must understand the strategic organizational goals and realize how business ethics can be applied through the available human resources (HR) of the organization. Practitioners must contribute to business success by developing rational policies. This indicates that there is a clear and fair vision, a set of integrated moral values, and a comprehensive code of ethics that fits into the present and future business needs. Human resources must know what is expected of them, they must understand the corporate goals, and most importantly their accountabilities within business operations. Ethics can provide workforce with commitment and motivation, while this positive attitude can enhance the implementation of rational policies.

Behave rationally is not just a simple action. For instance, optimality of mechanisms relies on the assumption that people behave rationally (according to their preferences), making the complexity of (optimal) mechanisms irrelevant (Huck and Weizsäcker 1999). Indeed, this process is limited by an individual's capacity to recognize, understand, evaluate, and react to complex conditions. A lack of ethics has been routinely displayed as a willingness to exploit corporate consumers, competition, investors, and employees for profit and the interests of the owners.

At this point, it is important to mention that the owner of an organization can be a single individual or a group of individuals. There could be a division of responsibilities between the board as being the chairman of the company, and the executive responsibility for business operations in terms of chief executive. These individuals are the representatives of shareholders. In terms of the latter, either there is one individual as the owner with 100 percent ownership or more than a single individual with a smaller proportion of shares, they elect their representatives such as the board of directors with executive and nonexecutive directors for corporations, and they hold the ultimate responsibility for their organizations' success or failure, and consequently, the implementation of ethical or unethical policies. Hence, claiming apologies after implementing such practices is not enough, either it is a single individual, an executive, or the shareholders of the legal entity. Business ethics needs policies that incorporate morals for the benefit of both corporate interests and human beings. In other words, having the capital to pay billions of dollars for fines and settlements due to various illegal activities does not give a corporation the permission to be unethical.

Human behavior includes limits to computational ability, willpower, and selfishness in the context of behavioral economics (Camerer 2014). This means that ethics borrows from neighboring sciences, such as norms (sociology), sociality (anthropology), psychophysics (theory about prosperity), and self-development and control (neurosciences). So, behaviors are mind-controlled, difficult to predict, and they can be affected by the environment in which an individual operates. Therefore, technology became very popular in recent decades because techniques such as machine learning allows instant or short-term exploration of many variables and defines new approaches where possible. Advanced and intelligent machines are doing tasks that no one expected were capable of being performed, while technology becomes embedded within businesses, societies, and even the human body, having a substantial impact on workplaces (Mantzaris and Myloni 2018). Additionally, the use of technology is inevitable in terms of coping with the risk dimension. Most of the financial decisions occur as a series of risks due to potential consequences of each decision. However, risk management is important not only in terms of financial instruments but also in the context of behavioral analysis and evaluation. Corporate policies can be described as important factors for eliminating such risks; however, provided that the use of the human factor is inevitable in many workplaces due to its unique characteristics, avoiding such conditions of risk is very difficult to achieve.

For instance, some human judgment patterns can be understood as imperfect by machine learning machines, thus the unstructured patterns expressed by human resources can be unreliable in an advanced, quite demanding, and competitive globalized business environment. For a human, more information input has a greater impact on confidence instead of better accuracy; while for an intelligent machine, it can result in greater predictive accuracy and increased efficiency. Additionally, many practitioners treat employees as a means to an end in terms of exploiting them to create value. However, this point of view can be evaluated from a twofold approach: either we can treat human resources as a mechanical part of an organizational system in terms of production in which people can be easily substituted due to a potential performance downturn, or we can take advantage of people's skills in order to create and add value to the corporate outputs by leveraging human's creativity, emotions, imagination, innovative ideas, senses, morals, and better understanding of what consumers (humans) actually need.

Machines form one part of the debate, while the other part is the employment of identical or near-identical biological copies of individuals, or in other words, clones. Reproductive cloning, as a practice of cloning a whole organism, such as a human being, to create a new individual is already a technological miracle of our age. Furthermore, some scientists believe that it would be ethically justifiable in at least some cases (Strong 2005). Additionally, therapeutic cloning, as the process of cloning pieces of deoxyribonucleic acid (DNA) or cells for therapeutic purposes, is partly legal in many countries, while reproductive cloning is strictly forbidden. Making human clones is unnatural. However, given that some corporations may promote unethical practices that are against human well-being, as they use people as a mere means, cloning could be a beneficial, efficient, and rational approach for creating an organism that has enabled its human-centered attributes instead of trying to develop artificial intelligence. Whether we agree on this, it could be our common future.

So, why is cloning worth mentioning in terms of business ethics and rational policies? Creating a genetic copy of an individual violates the right to genetic uniqueness. However, cloning or machine intelligence could be used over the exploitation of human beings as corporations would be legally able to employ such creations to increase social welfare. Thus, it is essential to develop business ethics in such a way they cover as much as possible of these emerged technologies and genetic capabilities. So, could a clone human being behave rationally and morally? If we believe that artificial intelligence is capable of moral behavior, which is already true in some cases, then yes, any entity would be able to implement moral practices and develop moral awareness. But, is it harmful for humanity to risk of having clones? Ethically, it could be very difficult to accept the process of creating human beings, particularly for increasing corporate productivity rates, rather than in cases when people cannot have biological children due to health reasons. People and corporations may accept this as an inevitable process of financial maximization and rational resource exploitation, but there will always be some individuals with several major arguments on this process.

Therefore, if it is in the best of our interest to employ third-party entities in order to produce goods and services, and given the existence of a universal and rational guide of strict policies on how to control this process globally, then business ethics cannot be against such a practice. However, considering that technology cannot eliminate the internal driving force of human willingness to work and create value, business ethics is more about human behavior and not about how machinery could exploit moral law. For instance, it is important to develop guidelines on how to control the collective or individual guilt in terms of entity responsibilities. Hence, we need fundamentals on how to make rational policies as an attempt to create a framework for human activity and utility in corporate environments, considering various dimensions and emerging challenges.

Ethics and Policy Relationship

Ethics and policy present a strong relationship in terms of their impact on each other. The process of policy making requires ethical awareness in order to conduct a moral set of principles, while the latter can be implemented only if there is a comprehensive set of moral policies. Additionally, ethical decision making can be influenced by codes of ethics, as they have a solid impact on the behavior of corporate agents (Schwartz 2001). Hence, ethics can be applied only by the existence of rational and moral policies, and vice versa. The goal of policy making is to guide individuals to produce rational outcomes. It can be concluded that policies are part of a general strategy that aims to develop and exploit organizational resources. Thus, a moral policy can facilitate and accelerate this process and lead to moral achievements.

A plethora of approaches exist in terms of policy-making methods: one of the most common and widely contested is the cost–benefit analysis (CBA) as a useful approach to compare the costs of providing the same beneficial outcome in different ways (Layard and Glaister 1994) and to estimate the strengths and weaknesses of alternatives in order to make a rational decision. In other words, this analysis provides the policy maker or the decider the essential tools to evaluate whether the benefits of a decision outweigh its costs. There are many other approaches such as the stages model, the behavioral decision theory (Edwards 1961), the punctuated equilibrium theory (PET) as a theory of organizational information processing (True, Jones and Baumgartner 2007), the rational choice theory (Boudon 1998), or the multiple streams framework theory (MSF). All these theories can be implemented in the context of ethics, considering multidimensional factors and the involved parties.

Policy is a course of action adopted or created by a policy maker, such as a government, a local community that is authorized to rule and control the public, or policy makers in a corporate environment, in response to different problems. A government regularly has several complex challenges as it must create a sustainable framework for each entity that belongs to a community in terms of law, economics, politics, environment, culture, and many more. However, given that the size of some companies is even greater than nations, in the context of their financial resources and impact on people, corporate policy making becomes even more important for society. Particularly, gigantic companies in the technology industry are larger than some countries of the world in terms of their annual revenues, financial and nonfinancial resources, and stock market value exceeding the sum of national income.

Therefore, policy is about making choices, while moral policy is about making ethical choices.

Consequently, the well-being and development of the global economy and of worldwide entities can have a significant effect on policy making. Undeniably, the economy as a concept of trading of goods and services in terms of exploiting comparative advantages of entities and individuals is a major driver for implementing ethical policies. When an economy or a set of economic policies are not performing well, other policy priorities such as ethics and how to behave morally are likely to become secondary. For instance, often when a financial crisis and depression occur, no community is capable of retaining its moral behavior due to the circumstances that deactivate their moral thinking process. Thus, when some conditions bolster negative corporate policies, such as strict productivity goals, efficiency rates that use human resources as mere means or the establishment of a corporate culture of punishment and strict work conditions, individuals cannot implement ethical activity even they have good intention to do so.

On the contrary, when an economy or a set of economic policies are performing well, individuals tend to either recover any losses of the past crises, while developing methods and ethical ways on how to avoid future turbulences, or exploit any resource available in order to achieve personal goals and serve individual interests, even if such an activity was unethical and irrational compared with other entities. Moreover, people tend to behave unethically even when they are worried that the financial situation could potentially trending downward just by following rumors, despite other rational solutions in terms of alternative partnerships and new investments. Therefore, business ethics and other sensitive issues such as environmental or societal policies are likely to be implemented when an entity can secure its financial sustainability. Policies incurring huge costs are usually among the first casualties of the decisions that do not consider ethics as their core element.

Policies are not isolated from the rest of the regulation and the importance of ethics as a stability factor. Indeed, many aspects are associated with policy making, whether they have a significant impact on the validity and fairness toward the entities involved. The feedback received during test and pilot times is essential for the development of a sustainable relationship between ethics and policy. Information and data gathered is always the best method of *moral entity consideration* as it enables individuals with engagement opportunities, while it supports policy makers of demonstrating ethical principles. Thus, multiple policies in different areas and issues can result in a comprehensive set of guidelines that play a critical role on how to behave rationally and ethically.

Policy-Making Fundamentals

Framing a moral and rational policy requires a multidimensional analysis of the objectives, planning potential strategies and alternatives, and considers the means to be used to achieve efficiency, given the available resources and environmental conditions. This process is crucial for the implementation of business ethics, and development of a moral awareness that must be strong enough to cope with corporate dilemmas depending on various factors and circumstances. In most cases, social and cultural values and norms drive policy makers to create frameworks that are compatible with societal perception and ethical fundamentals, even if people do not want to follow intentionally. For instance, if for a given community, a corporation that pollutes the environment during its operations is the only source of income for the people in the area, then most of them will ignore ethics in order to survive.

The policy-making process starts with the identification and definition of a problem. This initial stage of policy making is the most crucial as it forms the rest of the stages in a way that if the definition of a problem is based on incorrect information, then the policy will end up being incorrect as well, while it will have unethical consequences. Moreover, it is essential to recognize that problem solving requires a policy. Ignoring issues and circumstances cannot resolve a given problem, thus practitioners must be able to realize a situation and its conditions. Then, it is important to shape a set of approaches, improve past policies, and accordingly form a policy that secures development considering the various critical factors. It is not possible for policy formulation to eliminate the emergence of new problems and the presence of unprecedented conditions; hence, it is mandatory to debate during this stage of the policy-making process.

Consequently, policy legitimation and implementation are followed by policy evaluation as a process of information feedback that enables constant development and considers the consequences of policy implementation, as well as new ideas on how to make the policy even greater than its previous version. It is vital to remember that new challenges are always emerging, and in order to cope with those challenges and address new methods and policies to eliminate their negative impact on various factors, practitioners must find ways to make rational and ethical decisions, communicate the change to other involved parties, and how the latter will be influenced and motivated in order to implement such policies.

It is momentous to respect individual needs and concerns when making decisions affecting the beliefs, morals, positions, roles, prospects, or security of other entities. It is critical to provide equity and treat other individuals fairly, for instance, establish a work–life balance that enables individuals to deal with their personal and work obligations. Additionally, in terms of business ethics, working conditions must be healthy, safe, and pleasant for people, while the quality of working life must be satisfying, inspiring, and without pressure or stressful conditions that could negatively impact human resources.

One of the most important core policies is corporate determination to give equal opportunities to all individuals, irrespective of sex, gender, race, disability, age, marital status, or other specified conditions. For instance, it is worth noting whether there is a difference between sex and gender, as an notable part of corporate policies, when it comes to concrete conditions and job requirements. This is supported by the fact that many job positions are related to sex and gender requirements, so it is important to consider such criteria and be clear why you exclude alternatives. Many scholars distinguished between the two terms defining sex as the given biological differences between males and females, depending on one's sex organs, chromosomes, and hormones, while gender is about a choice, as some individuals decide to behave as being a female, despite being biologically a male, and vice versa. Through times, various theories have developed on how to avoid misunderstanding in terms of sex and gender differences, as sex is a biological fact, while gender is a social construction that can be untied from biology in some cases.

Thus, corporate policies must deal with this development as gender roles can change. Sex and gender can be easily confused as attempts to clarify the terminology have not been successful (Unger and Crawford 1993). In some cases, the two terms are being used interchangeably as synonyms, while in other cases the term sex instead of gender has become politically incorrect. For instance, scholars suggest including questions in data collection about sex at birth and current gender identity (Westbrook and Saperstein 2015). This is quite interesting in terms of corporate policies on data collection about their human resources and on how to ethically manage this set of sensitive data and accordingly the individuals themselves. Consequently, the use of "the terms sex when reporting biological factors and gender when reporting gender identity or psychosocial or cultural factors" is recommended, thus demographic and other data must be analyzed by sex, gender, or both (Clayton and Tannenbaum 2016, 1864), depending on policy requirements and goals, as well as the conditions on which the policy maker considers a set of variables. It is critical to develop a relationship of trust between the corporation and other entities.

Also, practitioners must treat employees equally in terms of their skills and qualifications, hence accept everyone's capabilities without direct or indirect discrimination. Furthermore, human resources can present some hidden capabilities; thus, it is important to consider their potential, rather than their current situation alone. However, it is essential to mention that even if a corporate policy is following this process of equality, this does not mean that the organization is aligned with ethics and meritocracy in each case. In many situations, people tend to treat some individuals more favorably under similar circumstances. This is a physiological process as the relevant legislation and codes of practice are not enough to eliminate an individual's internal beliefs, thus abolish bias in areas such as resourcing, promotion, pay, performance, and individual development. For instance, financial incentives can be a serious potential source of bias (Marnet 2005), so corporate policy makers should consider practices on how to eliminate such challenges.

Managing diversity requires much more than a degree or training certification. Hence, due to the complexity of a business environment and the characteristics of a community, there must be alternatives in policies that explain further approaches when a situation is not written in terms of a code of conduct and corporate policies. This suggests that a policy maker can implement rational discrimination decisions. In some cases, you can use rational factors such as when you want an individual with a degree in business administration for a specific job. It is not discrimination when a condition is positively correlated with a task that requires a specific set of knowledge, capabilities, and adaptive willingness.

In view of this, a corporation must develop and establish core policies to acknowledge cultural and individual differences in terms of their behavior and needs, thus utilize individual's talents, values, and norms to create a productive business environment. For instance, many studies stated that age requirements should not be set out on job advertisements. Petit (2007) suggested that age influences the probability of being invited to a job interview, leading to a significant hiring discrimination. If a machine with intelligent software was responsible for analyzing the application data of candidates and employees and then make the most rational decision on whatever a corporation needed, this problem could be eliminated. However, when a human is responsible for deciding, and even if the advertisement is according to the law and eliminates any discrimination issues, rational behaviors is less likely to be achieved at any stage of operations. Therefore, age discrimination cannot be avoided if a human decision maker cannot exclude his or her personal perceptions toward a rational decision.

Therefore, given the strong subjective feelings of humans, practitioners must develop their mindset capacity in terms of moral awareness, considering that we should respect the rights of other entities, reward them with equality and meritocracy, provide the opportunity for development, and advance flexible practices with respect to their personal life patterns and style. Accordingly, employees must behave in consideration of the same optimal business culture and act in the context of a discipline policy that informs employees on what is expected of them in work, and most importantly, what could happen if they violate corporation's policies. It is fair to demand more as a worker, but it is also important to behave in accordance with the principles of natural justice.

Consequently, it is worth noting that group rights must not eliminate individual rights. Particularly, a very complicated relationship exists between the rights of an individual and a group of individuals as it is often believed that whatever most people want to do is the best fit for everyone. However, this claim is not powerful enough to cope with alternatives. Practitioners should be able to find advanced methods and policies that can treat minority beliefs with respect. Larger groups and decisions made by the majority should allow room for improvement in terms of hearing what the minority believe and what new ideas could eventually increase the value of perceived policies. Thus, creating a stabilized corporate environment is a very difficult and demanding process, as it requires additional effort from all individuals and groups of individuals, in terms of finding a balanced point of reference, considering rational alternatives and ethical practices.

Additionally, it is not reasonable to implement someone's idea just to claim that you respect minorities, especially if this idea is insufficient for most people and entities. Also, it is not tolerable to legally restrict the freedom of individuals in the name of group solidarity. However, it is essential to evaluate all the alternatives and be cooperative in order to generate better policies and practices through a process of policy development with the given restrictions due to the available resources. Hence, minorities should attempt to understand and realize with respect whatever the majority wants, while the larger community could frame policies and make everyone's status better than before as they consider minority's alternatives that may could be more efficient in some cases.

The workplace as an environment that is governed by a set of policies and behaviors in a corporation must be inspired by a cooperative status that recognizes everyone's contribution. Making rational policies about challenges such as sexual harassment and bullying is essential for a corporation. However, making rational policies on learning how to avoid the existence and development of such issues is more important than just coping with them after their demonstration. Prediction of an individual's behaviors and making reasonable and good use of available data such as complaints and suspicious theories can be more efficient than establishing inflexible principles that cannot be applied under various circumstances.

Additionally, while business ethics is about the moral issues on the domain of an organization, we must be concerned about economic ethics as well in terms of the moral dimensions within the entire economy and social conditions. "Under conditions of competition, individuals cannot comply with moral norms in case this leads to higher costs which in turn leave them worse off than their competitors" (Luetge 2005, 110). Particularly, it is impossible to eliminate external factors in business operations, while it is also impossible to isolate an individual from his or her external environment. This implies that corporate policies cannot be sufficient enough if they do not reflect both the internal and the external environment in which the entities that the set of policies involves are operating. Thus, economic ethics, concerning the ethical outcome of economic policies, is an essential and fundamental part of policy making.

Different types of systems that are used by corporations in order to rationally exploit their resources and increase productivity have a strong impact on ethical awareness of their members and the society in which they operate. Since the ancient era, when Aristotle did not see ethics and economics as distinct disciplines, these aspects are closely intertwined. It is not about the Western societies or the perceptions of specific groups of people as globalization has eliminated most of the differences among economic models. In response to globalization and the increasing interdependence of global issues in the fields of economics, culture, politics, and the environment, global ethics and common moral norms emerged.

For instance, the 2008 financial crisis fueled globalization awareness, while the 2020 coronavirus pandemic triggered discussion on reversing globalization as it halted the economic activity and trade connections across the world through massive lockdown of workplaces and cities, resulting in the rise of nationalism, protectionism, and economic depression. Billions of people were being forced to evacuate public places and quarantine themselves as a strict and mandatory measure to protect human life over virus exposure. In both the situations, millions of people lost their jobs and unemployment rates increased dramatically, due to the enormous impact of the financial turmoil. Corporations had to react urgently on unpredictable conditions, while sometimes they did it by scarifying business ethics.

Globalization has a strong impact on applied ethics, on areas such as bioethics, labor ethics, and corporate social responsibility. For instance, globalization includes the development of methods on issues such as communication with colleagues from other countries; supervision of people with different culture; interaction with suppliers, consumers, and investors from all over the world; and management of a strategic plan, budget, and risk on a worldwide basis. Additionally, rights in various international human rights instruments are understood to be universal in nature, belonging to all persons by virtue of their common humanity (Chapman 2009). Hence, corporations often use universal policies; either they operate in the United States, Europe, Asia, or the South hemisphere. We are not in a world where there are city-states or country states anymore in the context of being capable of living and growing without trading with other entities and economies. In other words, we must exploit the comparative advantage of each country's resources in order to create a rational economic environment of constant development and well-being.

Corporations as part of the economy or otherwise stated as part of the sum of global financial entities, including governmental revenue and nonprofit institutions, must maximize their value in terms of serving their own needs and goals. It is worth noting that even nonprofit or nongovernmental organizations record revenues in order to satisfy their own needs, such as expenses for staff and facilities, though they work toward improving human welfare and the well-being of society. Particularly, the substantive vision of nonprofit and governmental organizations is usually described in terms of the mission of the organization and the activities the latter undertakes in the pursuit of the mission, though there are many similarities with for-profit organizations (Moore 2000).

Indeed, nonprofit organizations pursue the social and economic benefits of a positive and sustainable structural scheme, as well as reputation and social impact. However, as entities that are organized in terms of corporate structure are fundamentally focused on how to serve their own needs to retain a sustainable position in order to secondarily serve the consumers' and societal needs. Thus, corporate globalization as a process that removes some barriers to international trade, while others are constructed, allow the achievement of corporate goals and the rational exploitation of available resources for any form of organization. A global corporation is an added-value inventor and provider, while each company should find a unique added value in the context of differentiation over competitors (Sera 1992).

Hence, policy making is essential for the stability of an economic society as the latter cannot satisfy its needs without organized and structured entities such as corporations that are confronted with the making of goods and services. Determining who will do one task and who does another is a great challenge for corporate agents. However, policies must be developed in a way that they exploit competition, which fosters innovation and promotes the spread of new ideas and concepts. For instance, making products only as good as the competition forces to do could be characterized as an unethical practice, but at the same time quite common around the world, as organizations want to maximize profit ratio compared to competition, rather than produce the best product or service they can immediately.

There is a powerful connection between workforce behavior and corporate performance, and this can easily decrease the level of moral awareness of individuals. Therefore, practitioners must develop policies in terms of planning, organizing, leading, and controlling in order to ensure a work climate with ethical fundamentals that influence the behavior and activity of individuals. Employee empowerment can be achieved only through a relationship of trust, openness, growth, and consciousness. It is critical to increase employee satisfaction and team performance as an attempt to develop strong bonds between individuals and cope with legal, economic, political, cultural, and environmental challenges that have a significant impact on corporate operations and efficiency.

Concluding Remarks

Business ethics and rational policies are instruments that can enhance the survival of a corporation or lead to its failure. Having its roots back at least 2,500 years, business ethics has developed rapidly, while the behavior of individuals is being affected by ethical dilemmas and moral-related circumstances. Practitioners must develop their mindset capacity for *moral entity consideration* and adapt to change. Building a corporate governance system that enhances business ethics is one of the most important and demanding challenges. There is no universal method of policy making, while the latter is not isolated from the rest of regulation. Managing diversity is crucial for the work climate, and globalization plays a critical role by having a solid impact on applied ethics and corporate practices.

CHAPTER 2

The Critical Role of Human Resources

Business ethics is related to human decisions and directly connected with the standards and principles of fairness. Moral values are more than a simple element for a corporation. The ethical thinking of an individual is about to be forgotten in many cases, such as after the appearance of a financial turmoil or under the pressure of internal conflicts of interest. People in many cases tend to focus more on profits and financial returns, and less on business ethics and their moral identity. Consequently, without a universal moral environment, corporations must cope with additional challenges in terms of globalized competitiveness and international markets. Ethics is an opportunity to invest and develop the relationship between the decision-making center of an organization, its human resources, and its external environment, such as consumers, financial instruments, government, and the society in general.

Human resource management (HRM) is concerned with all business features of how human workforce is employed and efficiently managed in organizations. It covers a wide range of activities such as business ethics, corporate social responsibility, organizational development, behavior management, knowledge management, resourcing strategy, performance management, employee relations, and employee well-being. Guest (1987, 503) defined HRM as "a set of policies designed to maximize organizational integration, employee commitment, flexibility, and quality of work." HRM is about the maximum utilization of the human factor, as it is a vital resource accounting for any organization. The role of a human resource professional is much more demanding than the replaced term of personnel management. The latter was introduced into many large companies in a form of welfare capitalism, while the transition from personnel management to strategic HRM was a vital phase in the evolution of this field (Lundy 1994). The flexibility required and the diverged challenges of modern business environment mean that practitioners must focus on many factors previously been underestimated.

Therefore, respect for the individual is critical for business sustainability and moral development, while achieving success and organizational goals through people is a constant challenge for each corporation. Human resource professionals are accused by many academics and other critics of being manipulative and even unethical, as they exploit their human workforce treating them as mere means to the final output, without considering their status and moral-related issues. Manipulation through leadership is a more complex phenomenon than just one unethical way of acting (Auvinen, et al. 2013). This can be done through a variety of manipulation tactics, such as reason, charm, regression, coercion, silent treatment, and debasement (Buss, et al. 1987). Furthermore, exploitation, as a term that can be used to underline morally objectionable behavior, means that a human or an entity exploits another individual or an entity for the prior's interest by using unethical or even illegal practices. Thus, an organization can create a mechanistic formation as a hierarchical structure of control, authority, and communication through the implementation of an exploitation strategy to maintain a competitive advantage (Kehoe and Collins 2008).

As a good meaning term though, exploitation can be used to describe the inevitable process of organizing resources such as human capital, in order to enable their productive capabilities and create goods and services. In this sense, given an economic model that demands constant development and growth among nations, entities, and individuals, this good exploitation is not only a mandatory medium as a set of actions to achieve optimal efficiency and benefiting from resources but it is also the only alternative that corporations and individuals in general can use to achieve both organizational and personal goals. Therefore, it is not about capitalism. Wrongful exploitation such as harm, manipulation, or coercion will always exist, as it is in human's instinct, whether you call it capitalism, socialism, communism, or any other form of political governance.

Also, there is the term of mutual exploitation, as two or more individuals or entities exploit each other simultaneously. For instance, Marx refers to capitalism as a regime of mutual exploitation where both parties exploit each other in a single transaction (Wolff 1999). In business, this sort of relationship is expressed by the production on the one hand, and the reward to the labor on the other, such as an income and the infrastructure that is required in order to make the job easier and more efficient for labor. Still, this does not mean that both parties involved will have a positive outcome, as exploitation can have both positive and negative impact on either side. However, if each party realizes the reasoning behind an exploitative relationship, they would be able to present positive outcome and fairness. Thus, exploitation under concrete conditions could be beneficial for everyone. Instead of putting negative or positive tags on how to name a production system in a community, we must realize the available methods that capital holders must develop and implement to create value, or we must consider new ways or rules of optimal production.

However, developing a moral corporation and an ethical human workforce is not an easy task or a simple procedure. Each moment an individual decides, a moral issue is to be presented. While this action may harm or benefit others, each decision must have been revised multiple times instantly before the final act. If a decision has a moral component inside the frame where it belongs, it does not mean that this precise decision is a moral one. The critical role of human resources is about thinking before an action, and this process must be implemented each time individuals proceed with a decision, especially if it is crucial for the corporation or other entities.

It is important to understand that a human being may not be able to recognize that moral issues are at stake. Knowing which behaviors are ethical and which are not in order to adapt behaviors to ethical principles is not always possible. Thus, developing moral thinking skills is more important than applying traditional methods of ethics. A corporation has competence to determine the ethical rules complied with its practices, through its decisions, structure, policies, and business culture. The human factor in corporations has the critical role of exploring, implementing, and developing these principles, as the corporation is consisted by people working together for common goals and common beliefs of the outcome. Consequently, the stronger the moral identity of an individual, the more fairness will be implemented without being affected by immoral challenges.

If the governance system underestimates the ethical dimensions of human resources, particularly in times of financial crisis or other internal or external difficulties, then the corporation will be faced with legal and social reaction. The ethical dimension of HR management is crucial, as treating human individuals with moral principles must be a process of internal drive, and not due to legal requirements. Human resources must be treated equally, in terms of employment opportunities, rewards, and learning development options. They must be concerned with well-being features and avoid treating them as mere elements of production system. They are not just a part of the business chain; on the contrary they are the core of the system without which the latter cannot operate and produce value.

Automation and machinery implementations need the human factor as well in terms of initial production design and in order to consume the goods and services formed. A complete automated environment will never dominate current business models, eliminating human presence. Human needs lead many professionals to machinery options, due to challenges such as the protection of employees against harmful practices at work like bullying, harassment, and discrimination, as well as the need for providing a working environment that protests the health and safety of employees and minimize stress. Though the business environment is either not yet ready for 100 percent machinery exploitation, or humans do not want machines to take up all the tasks, mainly when these affect other people (Mantzaris and Myloni 2019). These expectations must be considered at the start of every corporate policy, as being moral requires a set of practices to this direction.

Human Resources beyond Strategy

Having a business strategy is a must for each corporation. Strategic management is critical for the maintenance and development of an organization, while human resources can be influenced by a great strategy. In this way, they can add more value to their efficiency rates and produce better results for the corporation and themselves as well. The main objective of a strategy is to achieve defined goals, and in order to do this, business ethics and human resources are two related crucial parts of the corporate plan. Business strategy is a systemic and connected mix of strategic choices, incorporating various strategies in terms of competitiveness, HRM, structure, technology, and finance (Boxall 1996).

However, is it possible to apply one common strategy? Is it feasible to integrate a strategy as a given within people in a corporation, thus follow a predefined tactic for any organizational procedure? The answer is not just a simple yes or no. Managing a business strategy, notably considering business ethics, requires a complex framework that recognizes the needs for each procedure, during each separate period. In addition, a comprehensive strategy must consist of the capability of a corporation depending on its resources, such as human resources, infrastructure, capital, and general internal policies. In some cases, it is quite hard to exploit both your workforce and other business sources, while implementing a moral plan.

To maximize the competitive advantage and achieve organizational goals a corporation must balance its capabilities with its environment. This demonstrates that human resources as the core of corporate success must be settled in the sense of associating business strategy with individual development. Making rational decisions have a significant impact on corporation, thus reorientation of strategies with business ethics can be beneficial for both individuals and organizations as entities. Indeed, a strategy can be regarded as a set of concepts, providing answers about how we can achieve something, given the various internal and external environmental conditions and characteristics, and what we want to accomplish.

The analysis of the internal environment can begin with the exploration of the key objectives of corporate strategy. This signifies that people within the organization must cooperate in an efficient way to achieve success through the enhancement and implementation of business core values, a fair responsibility distribution system, the employee value proposition scheme in terms of attracting and retaining high-quality people, concerns on how ethics can be part of daily behavior, and what characteristics corporate policies should have to ensure the engagement of human resources in the long term. The external environment relies on competitive pressure analysis, financial circumstances and economics in terms of market developments, reward trends, and policies, globalization as a high-weighted factor that has a strong impact on almost each aspect of a corporation, employment and legislation regulations, availability of skills, and finally demographic trends.

Hence, is it feasible to set up a strategy without a strong mindset stemming from human capabilities? Is it able to avoid the transformations in both internal and external environment, thus exploiting every time the available resources without challenges? Either it proved to be successful or disastrous, human resources are beyond a corporate strategy, as the responsible entity for implementing plans in order to achieve common goals by generating added value following corporate procedures. Individuals must feel that the corporate environment is a great, inspiring, and encouraging place in which they can work being happy, with value-oriented principles, enhanced ethics, plenty of opportunities for growth and development, and getting rewards based on recognized performance.

Therefore, human resources must be treated with fairness against any other valued entities in corporation. For instance, health and safety policies and practices, as programs that are concerned to deal with protecting the workforce and the other entities affected by organizational outputs, must be a priority for corporations. The prevention of accidents and minimization of incidents that result in hazards to people and/or property is essential for setting up a sustainable corporate environment. It is unethical to prioritize business needs and prevent individuals from demanding and exploiting ill-health- or work-related accident programs. Though there are many cost-related challenges in the corporate world, human resources are beyond profits and corporate financial assets, and business strategies must emphasize the health and safety policies as the ethical core of corporate climate in order to minimize potential losses.

So, is it ethical to let workforce suffering from lifting and carrying without providing the technological equipment required for their ease? Is it ethical to let people work under conditions where materials may fall, building maintenance is poor, machinery is outdated and not working? Also, is it ethical to exposure human resources to health hazards arising from operating machines without protective equipment or push them do repetitive strain operations that cause injuries or tell them to not stop working even if there is an emergent situation such as when an individual feels bad or there is a fire?

In addition, it is not ethical to measure how many million days are lost due to work-related accidents and ill health though analytics must include them to achieve better efficiency. It is not ethical to develop financial instruments and indexes that conceptualize human resources as corporate elements that need maintenance overtime, and that it is fair and reasonable enough to substitute them at any time due to human-oriented issues that lead to decreased efficiency. Corporations must create health and safety programs and a plan to carry out inspections periodically. Organizational policies must include processes such as identification and investigation of the causes of losses, then design of sustainable and feasible plans on how to cope with safety factors, and finally conduct a comprehensive and continuous program that educates and trains people on how to behave morally and safely in the work environment. Sabotage is at least unacceptable if not punishable. Harming other entities is a moral concerned issue that is expected in environments where the human factor plays a critical role. Hence, strategies must maintain good records and statistics about past incidents, in order to identify the frequency of issues, trends, and harming behaviors of individuals.

Considering this, employee well-being is a key factor for corporate success. People must be happy and well-treated in order to be productive for the organization and themselves. The feeling of satisfaction is very difficult to achieve. Though corporate policies must be capable of offering human resources the opportunity to improve their quality of working life, in terms of being motivated to contribute the most they are able to. Corporations must be concerned about the well-being of their workforce, not only because of their socially responsible programs, but also as part of enhancing human resources with commitment to the human value, fairness, and morally acceptable practices.

Another great example of the importance of rational corporate policies is harassment issues. Specifically, sexual harassment and racism incidents have always been two of the most controversial human-related challenges, while a proactive approach to preventing and remedying harassment as a corporate policy remains attainable for employers (Bland and Stalcup 2001). In terms of sexual harassment, as a repeated and unwanted behavior of a sexual nature between two individuals, in most cases it is difficult to prove it as there are not witnesses, while the victims are often unwilling to take (legal) action to avoid any further harassment. So, either it is a man's unethical action, or he was provoked by the behavior of the female, or the reverse is true, corporate policies must deal with the problem by implementing flexible but also strict and moral practices without preconception and discrimination. Additionally, we must make a clear distinction between actions that are harmful, and those that are acceptable by some people, but less tolerable by some other individuals. Generally, we need to be open-minded and less vulnerable to external behaviors, while we must develop and adhere to moral corporate guidelines regarding such incidents.

Human resources are beyond procedures, thus corporate policies against harassment and bullying cannot eliminate such practices just because they exist in a written form. Dealing with these issues is essential, by considering other entities and their rights, while ensuring that employees subjected to such harassment are given the opportunity to seek advice and that they can talk to someone freely and informally. These issues are quite sensitive, thus corporate policies must be aware of personal data, preferences, and personality differences. The establishment of a reporting procedure, and a comprehensive set of policies including protection of complainants and witnesses, as well as encouragement of victims to report the behavior to authorized individuals is very important.

Discipline, as a condition where individuals conduct themselves in accordance with the organization's policies and standards of acceptable behavior, must be developed in the context of an ethical work environment, not enforced by corporate agents. The organization must treat employees in accordance with the law and common rational principles. Handling disciplinary cases is difficult, given the cultural and individual differences in the workplace. Some of the factors to consider when implementing discipline policies include the seriousness of an issue, the duration of the problem and its frequency, the nature of the issue and whether corporate expertise is enough to cope with the problem, and the degree of its impact on other individuals and entities.

People are bringing their own perspectives and qualities to the work, thus corporate policies must employ strategies that can generate numerous sub-strategies focusing at one case per time, while actions must be fair and consistent with previous decisions in similar circumstances. Propositions such as work hard, you are late, do your job, and do not care about corporate policies, the tone and language used in formal or informal communication, or even the way individuals welcome each other in the morning, as a process of genuine concern for other individuals, are moral-related issues that are beyond pure performance and corporate status. Loyalty and commitment cannot be achieved through power and pay threatening. A disciplinary action must be immediate in response, corrective rather than punitive, while a progressive discipline approach with advance warning is usually more effective than a strict one.

Thus, it is very important to think before you act and consider a variety of factors before you behave, to avoid the creation of a negative work climate that is unproductive. At the same time, practitioners must be prepared to hear other individuals, in the name of employee voice. Ensuring fairness and consistency is always the goal for a sustainable corporate environment, while debates between employees must avoid nervousness and intense conflicts. Feedback is valuable only when it is shareable, in terms of accepting one's perceptions and thoughts, and be open to new ideas and different norms. Over the above, it is crucial to keep a history of the organization's discipline practices and consider how similar issues have been dealt with in the past. The process of making a policy, then enhance it with external feedback and expertise, accordingly implement it in terms of corporate practice, and finally evaluate the outcomes in order to re-strategize and reform practices that were weak or difficult to understand, is vital for organizational performance and the establishment of business ethics.

Moral Thinking through Education

From the early 1970s, when most countries came out from the post war environment and finally they had the essential resources to promote a comprehensive educational system as a mandatory part of human's life, they tried to develop educational frameworks to provide young people with a series of values and sciences, including moral education. This process is still very challenging, as each moral developer can share his or her own ethical perceptions and different points of view. The consolidation of education was not only a great start for enhancing a peaceful environment among nations, but it was a prime option for a state if the government wanted to secure a rational growth pace of its society and people. Ethics cannot only be transmitted through the family or the church, as it was believed in the past, particularly in cultures with solid religious beliefs. There is no particular batch of the content, teaching method, or configuration of students and space that will accomplish our ends in terms of moral education (Noddings 1994).

Moral development and ethics have always been a very important part of education. However, since the widespread of the value of learning, most people were not able to recognize the significance of education toward human behavior and interpersonal skills, which is still an issue in some cases. Regularly, people do not encounter moral principles and ethical behavior consideration in their formal education. Hence, lacking the necessary and crucial educational background for business ethics, they cannot implement this concept on their daily routine, making for an organization more difficult to develop a sustainable and creative business culture. Globalization has created an environment in which education is critical for everyone, as this internationalized corporate world involves linkages between local, regional, national, and global scales of economic, political, social, and environmental issues. The speed of this process is associated with additional challenges for individuals, considering that business ethics must be reoriented each time an innovation and new knowledge emerges.

This implies that the consequences of interventions cannot just be analyzed under a theoretical base. But they must be conceptualized into new forms of training needs. In principle, technology and globalization offer an unprecedented stream of knowledge, enabling the potential of widespread education through common rules and corporate policy requests, though it could lead to the elimination of some local characteristics. The richness of training dimensions leads many practitioners to reevaluate the need for additional and lifelong training through all corporate procedures. Given that time management is crucial for everyone, moral thinking through education must be developed in such a way that the learner can develop his or her own ethical principles internally, without the need to apply guidelines.

The process of the internal *moral entity consideration* starts with a core force about implementing business ethics. An individual cannot be able to apply ethics because he or she must do it, or after a short time of attending educational programs. Academicians and mentors cannot transfer the ability of moral thinking through a single knowledge lecture or lesson, even if they are field experts. They do not have the ability to motivate learner's moral instinct, not because they do not have the knowledge to do so, but due to difficulties of individual learning level, when the training contains sensitive concerns, such as ethics and values. You cannot teach someone how to implement business ethics. Instead, you can initiate an individual to the concept of moral thinking.

Furthermore, education must consider globalization as a major influencing factor to its fundamentals. Training policy must identify global assignments, cross-cultural needs and requirements, local characteristics, and thus develop a program that covers both general and specific cultural orientations. Hence, knowledge management is crucial for developing rational corporate policies, as organizations that do not practice knowledge management can record a competitive disadvantage. Knowledge management is the systematic underpinning, observation, instrumentation, and optimization of the corporation's knowledge economies (Demarest 1997), or in other words a process of capturing, organizing, and storing information and experiences of individuals, and making it available to others. Also, the motivation for learning must be strong enough in order to achieve knowledge management optimization. This suggests that whether an individual is motivated by expectations or goals, corporate policies must support educational and training programs in terms of motivating people to self-development. Thus, an individual can be motivated by expecting moral behaviors and a fair role and reward feedback on achieving something desirable for him or her, and by setting morally achievable goals that enhance individual contribution.

Educational systems must be followed by post-hoc actions such as knowledge capturing, documenting, storing, sharing, transferring, and reevaluating of information. Knowledge is multi-faceted and complex, situated and abstract, implicit and explicit, distributed and individual, developing and static, verbal and encoded, and an active process that is mediated, provisional, pragmatic, and contested (Blackler 1995). Explicit knowledge can be recorded and held in databases, while individuals are the primary repositories of tacit knowledge (Haldin-Herrgard 2000). This type of knowledge is obtained by internal individual processes. We need education and lifelong learning; however, a part of knowledge cannot be reached and trained in closed doors. It is not possible to teach an individual to have talent or experiences. The gaining of experiences could be done at a mind level, only if the individual is reasonably capable of leveraging knowledge in combination with creating multidimensional intellectual environments through his or her mind capacity. This process though is quite demanding, thus only a small fraction of people can cultivate.

Moral thinking must be an internal process that has been emancipated from principles and rules for action in terms of coping with demanding and unprecedented challenges. Education must provide a wide and diversified portfolio of knowledge, creating a theoretical background useful to understand the change and environmental variables. Due to difficulties in sharing tacit knowledge, business ethics must be written in the context of a code of ethics and be shared through various communication channels between individuals. Personal beliefs and perceptions, in most cases, prevent people from accepting ethics and knowledge without questioning about them or building doubts about their reliability. There is no common practice to force someone to believe and to adopt knowledge. If an individual does not want to follow a script, then no one can change his or her mind and perceptions. However, through people-oriented tools, it is possible to achieve growth of ethic awareness of other parties.

If you treat other people as the medium to accomplish organizational goals, making them pieces of the mechanism, and not part of business culture, ethics cannot be achieved. Instead, moral thinking must be developed at a personalized level, with strategic knowledge inputs, thus generating moral perceptions and behaviors. Also, everyone in the corporation must be encouraged and given the opportunity to develop their ethical skills. Everyone must be able to maximize their capacity of moral thinking. Practitioners should promote a learning culture and education as a priority for each one of the individuals in order to success. Corporate policies must include recognition and rewards for those who have the willingness to keep on learning and find ways to motive the other individuals that are not interested in education, presenting a stable or declining direction to their knowledge levels.

Learning, as a process of constructing new capabilities, skills, and knowledge, is essential for both individuals and the corporation. Either it is an individual's willingness to learn more or the organization requires new skills, both terms referring to one common goal, that of making an individual's mind and capabilities better with various methods, in order to achieve personal and team goals. Thus, the encouragement of learning is limitless. Indeed, it is a lifelong process that consists of valuable resources for all entities. For instance, a workplace can be a learning environment. This highlights that a variety of on-the-job training is happening, while the individual must absorb various environmental factors in order to increase performance and mental level.

People behave considering their perceptions, needs, and expectations of other entities such as a corporation or their colleagues. Education as a set of predefined or unsettled norms cannot cope with real-time behaviors universally. Norms are the unwritten rules of behaviors that are not formed as policies or procedures. Hence, individuals must extend their educational and learning capacity in order to develop their internal driving forces of morality, through structured plans on what they need to be trained, what they must learn to be efficient, what the corporation needs by its human resources, and how training and learning is possible, in terms of finding the right educational methods.

Some people can learn with the use of e-learning and web-based technologies through their computers and personal devices. Other people prefer traditional educational methods, such as a classroom, and someone to guide them as a coach or mentor, in shorter or longer educational segments. Mentors provide people with specific advice and guide them with learning programs and on how to acquire the necessary knowledge and skills, not only to individuals that are in the early stages of their careers, but to people that need an advice on dealing with any kind of problem such as technical, administrative, or even at a personal level, anytime throughout their career life. Other people need to have an experience or to simulate a situation in order to learn new things. Many individuals need to be part of a team to concentrate, while others need to stay alone and explore things out for themselves, else they are getting distracted. Also, there is a minor category of individuals that can make their own educational paths through self-directed learning techniques. This self-initiated process is efficient for individuals that are capable of planning what knowledge they need, as if they overestimate their capabilities then this self-plan could end up with negative results.

It is important to mention that a combined method as blended learning may could be the best learning plan, as both education and experience are essential. However, education alone cannot ensure practicality under all circumstances and operations, while experience may be repeated many times, and thus be unable to offer development. In other words, an individual working for a corporation at a similar position doing comparable tasks for many years is stable, as this could be analyzed as the same little experience, repeated many times through years of work. Therefore, education and learning in general is important, due to its continuous level of development in the context of a variety of factors such as technological, financial, social, and environmental progression.

In any case, whatever the education channel that is preferable, moral thinking is taking place with the consideration of the impact and consequences that an action might have to other entities. This self-motivated consideration is essential for applying business ethics, thus contributing to the creation of a moral corporate culture. Furthermore, corporations must develop policies that analyze the perceptions and behaviors of individuals, and then relate them to corporate development needs, set goals, prepare a rational action plan, and finally implement a comprehensive strategy as it was established. The development of a corporation is important, but this can only be efficient through developing people. So, practitioners are responsible for unveiling these attributes and improving operational flexibility by extending the range of skills needed as a successful and sustainable corporation needs a lot more than just human workers who get the work done.

Having strong education and training programs is not enough. A corporation must ensure through its policies and procedures that individuals have applied their learning on their work environment and operations. The impact of changes in their behavior within business operations could be extremely effective for any business function. Additionally, the corporation must benefit from learning programs, in the event of corporate growth, performance, and sustainability. Time should be allowed for the change in behavior to take place, as moral thinking and generally learning a new skill is usually difficult to adopt instantly.

Learning and education do not consist of a race between people. Individuals are unique, and they have different intellectual levels and understanding capabilities, thus it is not fair to push everyone with the same pressure level. Some people may satisfy business needs faster than other individuals. The learning process is related to several factors, such as the internal drive to learn, the individual's personality, and the responsiveness level, in the context of developing appropriate actions that lead to effective behaviors and performance. Additionally, organizational learning capability can be defined as processes which enable flow of knowledge (Deshpande 2012). So, claiming an ethical identity is impossible to be achieved without proper actions. Behaving morally for yourself, while your activity is unethical for others is not the right to do either.

Summarizing, moral thinking through education is a reachable goal, and corporate policies must consider various critical factors. First and most importantly, people have emotions. As a result, emotional respect, engagement, and management are crucial for the implementation of corporate policies. Many times, emotions limit our learning pace, while this process can have a negative impact on what we have learned already. A strong and powerful experience, or an accident, a quote or a sentence on a scientific book can alter our points of view on many dimensions. This can create new emotions and thoughts on the same circumstances, while it can modify our thinking process substantially. Indeed, we can learn better in stimulating environments and by interaction, while our brain needs time to reflect to embed the learning. Furthermore, the aging of our brain is very important, and it needs additional attention. We cannot maintain our learning abilities and maximum learning pace throughout life, as "advancing age is paralleled by a reduction of the ability to acquire new skills, impacting social and professional life" (Zimerman, et al. 2012, 10).

In the past, most people thought that education is for young people only. Then, business needs for additional skills since the first industrial revolution led people to supplementary education, while in recent decades, the concept and process of lifelong learning was developed and altered most people's perceptions. At this point, it is essential to mention that moral education is very challenging to teach, as educators must be capable to distinguish their personal moral values from the educational process. This means that a learner must have the opportunity to freely develop his or her moral thinking capacity and skills by responding to the received information over ethics, and form an individual concept on how to think and behave ethically. Educational systems must provide people with multidimensional schemes and approaches that enable personal interventionism. This is particularly critical for practitioners and individuals who are going to be committed to serving organizational interests.

Business ethics is not simply a set of moral behaviors documented in order to be a practical guide on how to behave ethically. Business ethics as a set of values and moral principles have also an educational purpose. In the context of rational corporate policies, business ethics must be able to provide a vision, and influence individuals on how to behave ethically against their internal force of egoism and the feeling that serving self-interest is the only purpose of a human being. Moreover, knowing that you carried out an unethical action against another individual must not be a pleasant feeling. Education and learning channels such as part of corporate policies must be able to promote the development of moral thinking, in a way that the individual cannot internally accept behaving unethically, notably when the action and its consequences involve other entities.

The Commitment to Value

The meaning of value considers the regard that something is held to deserve. The importance and usefulness of a material, the monetary worth, and the principles of behavior of an individual entail that value is fundamentally a crucial element of comparing two or more conditions. Furthermore, it is a vital part of the evaluation process, while it creates an environment of motivation, and enables individual willingness to generate value. Additionally, ethics, as an important branch of knowledge that deals with moral principles and governs individual behavior, is superior to law. The latter is formed by the government as a minimum standard for individuals and entities in terms of implementing legal policies and making decisions that follow regulation. However, being ethical implies that an individual considers significantly more values than just the minimum required in order to be legally acceptable.

One of the most widespread questions concerning ethics is about what money can buy, and what cannot be negatively affected by monetary value. We can recognize that in practice, in some cases, money-driven individuals can be satisfied with monetary benefits, and they can put aside ethics and their moral values given the condition that they are secured from being caught, or that their action is at least legally aligned. This is critical, as a legal activity, even if it not ethical, can be used as an excuse for third-party entities or in order to satisfy internal awareness and instinct motivation. However, we must seek to approach what money can buy without involving emotions and moral viewpoints during this process. First, the commitment to value in terms of money means that an individual's integrity can be flexible enough in order to be inspired and influenced by money forces. Thus, the level of respect that individuals feel can be altered, as an attempt to exploit any given opportunity and take advantage of the monetary benefits. Trust can be modified as well, because those individuals will consider that an action that can generate money is the one that has to be implemented.

Therefore, people relations can be money-oriented, and individuals can change their trust levels toward other individuals, depending on money-driven values, aiming for more profit. The one who will gain his or her trust is the individual who will provide more money. This simple rule in the money world can generate a plethora of unethical activities because the use of money to gain the advantage of resources and individuals is the easiest method to exploit their vulnerable behavior. Accordingly, considering the critical role of human resources in business, commitment to money can be both a valuable and a disastrous part of daily operations. Corporations are established in order to deliver products and services as a mean to generate profit, as an essential part of a set of values including work conditions and people engagement. Thus, individuals that are committed to make money, can be useful in business operations such as negotiations with suppliers or consumers, and in terms of the structure of corporate monetary policies. Their extended mindset capacity in the context of creativity as an attempt to explore methods on how to generate value can be very important for organizational innovation and development, and vital for corporate sustainability.

However, their willingness to gain more, without *moral entity consider-ation* as their primary principle of thinking on decision making, can create the conditions of a stressful work environment, in which their monetary interests must be satisfied with practices that are against other individuals or even the organization they work in. Having a solid work ethic in corpora-tions generating a huge amount of money and value in general is critical against bribery, fraud, and extortion. There are undoubtedly several meth-ods for violating morals and standards of doing business. At the same time, you cannot buy the honesty of an individual, so it is possible to be deceived in the name of money. Although a business can adopt policies opposed to such practices, human instinct to serve his or her own interests means that it is almost impossible to control the overall of such behavior in corporations.

Another important statement is that some people claim that money cannot buy someone's ideas. However, in practice, money can not only buy ideas but it can exploit them with unethical practices as well. For instance, a startup company is a legal way to translate an idea into the corporate world in order to develop scalable business models. Though, there are two considerable approaches on this sort of business. On the one hand, some entrepreneurs name a new corporation as a startup one, just for exploiting capital and funding programs promoted for innovative ac-tivity because a startup must be primarily characterized by its innovative operational mission. Thus, people exploit this wave of investment on in-novative ideas in order to serve their individual interests, even though the established business does not present any innovative characteristics at all. Additionally, they do not have any intentions to grow the startup beyond the initial scheme, so they attempt to attract investments in the short term without securing long-term and large-scale business sustainability.

On the other side, some people build and develop their startup models considering business ethics, so they put additional effort to secure sustain-ability and growth in the long run. Also, they develop ideas into practical goods and services, and they consider the feedback in order to validate that they follow a critical path of maximizing value, with accuracy, focus, and knowledge gain. But, when the commitment to value substitute ethics with money-driven forces, this could be disastrous for the busi-ness models developed. This means that larger corporations may acquire smaller companies, such as startup ones, in order to exploit their business model. Though this process confirms that the mission of a startup is accomplished, it can have a negative impact as well. Some entrepreneurs buy startups and in general other smaller companies and their ideas, patents, concepts, and other copyrighted material because they want to prevent the development of such goods and services in the name of profit and personal interest. For instance, it is unethical but also profitable to prevent the development of a business model that makes the production of a good or service more efficient by decreasing its cost, as it could generate less profit due to competition forces. Particularly, entrepreneurs would be willing to eliminate such models, in order to prevent of being pressured to decrease the price of their goods and services due to competition or change their business model and operations, while other businesses cannot exploit those ideas due to the rights that the first has acquired.

The process of silencing ideas satisfies individual interest; however, it prevents social growth and well-being given the available resources. Hence, it is not about what money can buy and whether an individual is capable of exploiting someone's vulnerability, but it is about how people can develop their mindset capacity in the context of ethics, and whether they can evolve a compelling character with limited fluctuations. Being rational is easy for most people in terms of serving their own interests. But, on the contrary, being ethically rational is feasible only if the condition of objectivity is achieved. Human resources can be objective if they are not influenced by personal feelings or other circumstances in considering various facts. This is a quite demanding procedure and requires concrete skills of avoiding being subjective. Thus, making objective judgment is crucial for the implementation of business ethics, while corporate policies must include objective terms as well. The commitment to value can be translated into a powerful strategic tool, however if you cannot distinguish whether you must be subjectively rational, then your commitment and loyalty levels cannot be aligned with moral principles.

Concluding Remarks

Business ethics is associated with human resources, their decisions, and behaviors. Achieving success and organizational goals through people is a constant challenge for each corporation. Wrongful exploitation such as harm, manipulation, or coercion will always exist, hence practitioners must adhere to corporate policies that enable individual development and enhance the critical role of human resources. There is no universal strategy, while a comprehensive plan must consist of the development capability of a corporation depending on its resources, particularly in terms of implementing moral practices. Employee well-being is a key factor for organizational success, and corporate policies must be proactive against issues that could have negative impact on work climate, such as harassment or discipline. This includes the promotion of education as a vital practice to increase the moral mindset capacity of human resources. This is feasible through a variety of educational channels, and this process could be catalyst as an attempt to cope with the commitment to value. Money-driven individuals can be proved as a critical factor for the downturn of a corporation, and efficient business models must be developed rather than silenced.

PART II

Moral Organizational Development

This part deals with some of the most important business ethics instruments, such as corporate social responsibility, the code of ethics, the agency theory, and the aspects of leadership and management. It describes the fundamental features that associate the characteristics of human resources to business ethics and moral practices, it examines the ethical dimensions of different types of administration and employers, it provides a moral compass for the role of individuals in the corporation, the concept of an ethical business philosophy through a rational corporate social responsibility, and it clarifies what is a moral attitude in the context of individual well-being.

Ethical corporations treat people with respect, honesty, meritocracy, and integrity. This is very important as an attempt to keep promises and high commitment levels while implementing the business plan and achieving organizational goals. Business ethics is concerned not only with internal corporate operations but also with external interconnections, such as interactions with consumers, investors, and government.

CHAPTER 3

Rational Corporate Responsibility

The word "responsibility" refers to the state or fact of having a duty to deal with something or of having control over someone, as a state or fact of being accountable and the responsible for blaming when something happens. "Corporate social responsibility is the notion that corporations have an obligation to constituent groups in society other than stockholders and beyond that prescribed by law or union contract" (Jones 1980, 59–60). Business ethics are interconnected to the dimensions of corporate social responsibility (CSR). This implies that the decision makers of a corporation are authorized to take actions, considering the well-being of individuals and the good of society, in order to achieve organizational goals.

CSR is a corporate dimension of actions that takes account of the social, economic, legal, ethical, and environmental impact of how an organization operates (Table 3.1). The latter as an entity, or in other words as an artificial corporate individual that is legally created, is responsible for the rationale of corporate policies, in the context of the integration of moral corporate systems, the implementation of legal requirements, and

Table 3.1 *Corporate responsibility framework*

Core responsibilities	Societal responsibilities
• Secure a sustainable business environment. • Be profitable and create value for both employees and stakeholders. • Provide goods and services with accountability and secure business standards. • Implement policies according to law and regulation.	• Produce healthy goods and services and do not harm. • Consider societal and environmental needs and modify business outputs accordingly. • Support societal values, ethical codes, norms, and principles. • Do moral philanthropy, not philanthropic marketing.

the overall consistency of its procedures. Sustainable corporate policies emphasize that corporate responsibility must be a top priority under all business functions. Moral actions are directly associated with corporate sustainability. Regarding an approach of mutual enhancement of responsibility, the more the corporation is responsible, the more the individuals become responsible and vice versa, while finding a balance between corporate culture and individual behavior is critical (Constantinescu and Kaptein 2015). The broader range of obligations that corporations have toward society beyond maximizing profits is embedded in the conceptual framework of CSR.

Organizations must operate by securing long-term economic performance by avoiding short-term social and environmental wasteful behaviors (Porter and Kramer 2006). Indeed, many corporations ignore their social obligations, stating that these are not of their business responsibilities. However, successful corporations need a general system of development in terms of education, innovation, health care and the consideration of people needs, and fair treatment for individuals as an integrated and not distinguished part of a healthy society. Only then the workforce could be productive, motivated for work, and devoted to organizational and personal goals. Hence, CSR is the process of applied ethics that a business must consider in order to serve social and corporate expectations.

There is a distinct relationship between the corporation and its policies with the issues concerning the society in which it operates. For instance, the emergence of multinational corporations led them to include in their CSR programs a global corporate citizen philosophy (Cacioppe, Forster, and Fox 2008), as there are factors that have strong worldwide impact, such as concerns about the global environment. A corporation must be aligned with law, financial and other government regulatory, supply chain and pricing practices, have transparent procedures ruled by internal and external supervisors, be able to give equal opportunities to everyone, provide safe working conditions, have fair compensation policies and rewards, develop policies on diversity and discrimination, demonstrate procedures regarding privacy and data management while handling rationally the products and obsolete items.

Also, it must have an enhanced environmental awareness such as for recycling, waste, energy and water usage, emissions, and utilizing natural and technical resources. Corporations must develop strategic motives as they are crucial for adopting an environmental CSR focus (Babiak and Trendafilova 2011). However, integrating corporate and social needs under the same policy program needs more than an agent's or a shareholder's good intensions. Being ethical toward society is a continuous and very demanding process. Practitioners need to prioritize corporate needs and place them harmoniously into social expectations. They must choose which social issues to focus on, while not ignoring the other they cannot focus due to their position or available resources. Value-driven management and leadership are associated with both economic efficiency and a great number of ethical values. Morals are not only subject of internal behavior but they also reflect the ethical identity of the organization toward society and other entities. Hence, it is essential for a corporation to develop a moral vision, related to shared values and perceptions.

For instance, corporate philanthropy is a significant start, but this is not enough as an attempt to be characterized as a social contributor. Corporations and their people must behave with ethical commitment for improving general quality in a community. Thus, if the corporate policy is to set high prices to its goods and services, to maximize financial return, and then to promote and implement social responsibility programs, this process can be criticized from rather different perspectives. Some people may want lower prices on goods and services, as an opportunity to offer help and philanthropic actions to other entities by themselves. On the flipside, other people may need to centralize social responsibility behavior by giving large companies in private sector the authority to do such activities, even if the cost for this process is higher price tags of the provided goods and services.

In any case, corporations must develop their policies in the sense of fairness and meritocracy, considering the rights of others. If the resources of a corporation are not enough to implement CSR programs, then policy makers must find ways that do not require spending money at all. For instance, companies with low budget can make decisions and operate in a way that does not harm others, so without additional cost they can have a moral CSR program. Indeed, most businesses around the world are preferring this kind of action to deal with their social image. Most people are waiting from larger corporations to develop and implement social programs, thus entry-level and medium enterprises usually avoid applying such practices, as they feel unable to provide a comprehensive and sustainable policy. But, by avoiding corporate moral obligations in the name of cost or other factors, it makes some businesses present a decreased sense of ethical awareness.

Given the multidimensional demands of the society and human beings, it is impossible to fulfill each desire. Corporations and their policies should not attempt to create lists of community desires, in a short-term base, unless there is a current need or situation that their help could be critical, thus they must present flexibility. Instead of temporary policies, CSR programs must have a vision for the future. Policy makers must take actions that are aligned with law and ethical minimum that is regulated with common rules by the community or government. At the same time, they must develop a wide range of activities, in terms of seeking solutions to broader societal issues, such as health improvements in the context of human well-being, support a precautionary approach to environmental change, or actions against unfair low wages, poverty, and the spread of discrimination in the work environment. Hence, it is essential to comply with laws and regulations, it is critical to make strategic and rational decisions beyond legal duties, while it would be great if a corporation has the resources needed to develop programs that support the local and broader community in which they operate as a set of practices that promote and implement enhanced corporate moral obligations.

Responsibility Defined

The implementation of a CSR program could be characterized as a process of dealing with conflicting interests. This indicates that practitioners must cope with rather different approaches on business ethics and morals of a given community as an attempt to develop policies to approach a balance point that it is fair for all the involved parties. Therefore, before moving to the next step of applied CSR activities, it is essential to develop a comprehensive method to explore what actions are required in the context of ethics and social responsibility, how the corporation can support and develop such activities and with what resources, evaluate the impact of the program toward both the organization itself as an entity and the community in which it operates, and finally explore how it is possible to retain the implementation of such ethical activities. In other words, it is necessary to define the level of corporate responsibility toward other entities and develop procedures in order to implement such strategies.

CSR is measured by following a business organization's configuration in the context of principles of social responsibility, processes of social responsiveness, and outcomes of social responsibility (Hopkins 2005). Although there is no universal set of specific guidelines to define the CSR level, policy makers can develop such activities through a process of questioning about a series of crucial issues. At first, it is important to consider corporate annual turnover, the organizational structure and needs, the number of employees and their rights, and the position of the corporation within the industrial sector. This is critical as CSR programs can record a wide range of practices to implement, as the corporate size, financial condition, available resources, and human capital in the context of generating ideas and participating in such activities can be well diversified between rather different corporations.

Then, it is important to address the motives and reasons for the corporation and its people to engage in CSR policies. Given the available resources, corporate policies can be developed in such a way to serve rationally both corporate mission and society expectations. A corporation cannot exist as an autonomous entity and ignore the needs and expectations that other individuals and entities have toward the corporation as a member of a community. Similarly, the latter cannot overlook the fact that corporations are established in order to serve their own interests as well, as shareholders take the risk of investing capital as an attempt to develop wealth and make profit from the value that corporate resources and outputs can generate. Thus, practitioners must explore the alternatives, evaluate the expectations from different points of view, make critical decisions in terms of the volume and degree of CSR engagement, and conduct a set of activities that are sustainable and valuable for both corporation and society.

At this point, it is vital to mention the reasons that make a CSR program valuable. Individuals, in the name of a corporation as a legal entity, can develop their responsibility level and moral awareness as a process of increasing their ethical norms and making the existence of the corporation important for the society and people in general, and not only for money-driven individuals. This process can improve financial performance as well, while the commitment levels can be enhanced alongside with the brand value and corporate reputation. An effective CSR program can reduce operating costs and increase productivity because conducting such a policy attracts investors and long-term partnerships, while the corporation can secure good relations with the communities and the government. This makes the corporation more sustainable than before, they exploit and increase their competitive advantage, and it enables them to be associated with additional reputation channels, such as making the brand name as the corporation standard in the industry. This can be insightful for other smaller, similar, or even larger-size companies, while individuals will be willing to be part of a corporation with this level of commitment and engagement.

Thus, the legitimacy of a CSR program can be indicated through the code of ethics, the public responsibility through activities including job creation, contribution to innovation, and regulation compliance, while corporations must develop mechanisms to review social issues relevant to them, evaluate internal issues such as industrial relations and policies, and generate responsible outcomes in terms of social contribution. Hence, the process of questioning provides practitioners a guide on what issues are most important for the corporation and the community, aiming at the creation of a solid, ethical, and fair CSR set of activities. Defining the responsibility of a corporation through critical questions on important issues can be described as a process of internal interview. The difficult part of this process is to be morally fair and honest in order to report not what you would want to answer, but what happens in practice. For instance, among the most critical questions is about the case of employee layoffs. Reporting the causes for these reductions with fair treatment to workers is vital, as practitioners must identify their responsibility when they substitute people for reasons such as the profit, rather than skills or other conflicting interests. The establishment of rational corporate policies means that practitioners recognize their actions in a fair manner, and then alter their behavior in order to implement practices characterized by meritocracy, fairness, and consistency with respect to CSR reporting.

Accordingly, as individuals have their own portion of responsibility, the level and volume of employee involvement in corporate decision-making procedures is crucial. In terms of labor relations, employee involvement shows whether corporate policy and decision makers consider employee voice, which can be translated as an important part on developing corporate responsibility activities. The latter do reflect not only the brand image toward the external environment but also the practices within its internal environment and workplace.

Practices such as to enhance health and safety policies in the workplace; treat employees fairly in terms of work hours, compensation, and benefits; provide training and skills development; respect for multicultural individuals, minorities, and diversity; provide individuals with fair opportunities; and generally to serve the needs of employees are very important CSR activities. Pretending to be a moral employer and at the same time treating internal issues with unethical methods is two times more unethical than trying to be moral when the resources available are not enough to implement practices for external activities. In other words, business ethics has its initial point of reference on internal procedures, and this leads to present an ethical set of activities to the external environment as well. For instance, when a corporation invests to increase the use of renewable energy sources in terms of energy efficiency for its own operations or the level of recycling and reuse, this can be a positive CSR activity for both the internal and external environment.

Therefore, is it possible to conceal an internal corruption or bribery issue as an attempt to avoid responsibilities? Is it possible to receive donations by a third-party entity in order to not unveil an unethical practice or report it to authorities? Is it possible to set profitability as a priority above all other considerations, such as health and safety of employees and consumers? Indeed, many corporations cannot satisfy the above ethical requirements in the name of decreased available financial resources, or avoid taking responsibility by blaming specific individuals for their unethical behavior, such as members of the management. For this reason, it is essential to develop rational corporate policies and codes of behavior, in order to be able to identify who is responsible, and what procedures will be implemented to eliminate such behaviors and practices. These procedures must be shared through all internal corporate communicational channels as a process to define ethical subjects and enhance corporate values.

Policy makers are responsible for developing a series of essential guidelines to promote important ethical principles. In practice, there is a vital relationship between the corporation, the society in which it operates, and the government. This implies that governmental intervention can be a determining factor on developing CSR programs as business initiatives must adhere to legal requirements and rules by following the highest international standards. At the same time, people forming a community can have strong impact on corporate decisions, as they are consumers, employers, suppliers, or other professionals. Additionally, human resources have a fundamental role in business activities. They are responsible as individuals or as a team toward a wide range of issues concerning corporate activity. Hence, unethical practices could mean that consumers would stop buying your goods and services, potential employees would not be willing to be part of your company, while current workers would want to leave, suppliers would lose their trust and withdraw any financial connections with the corporation, and other professionals would not want to associate their name and career with such unethical corporate practices.

Therefore, it is very important to retain a balanced and multidimensional relationship between businesses as legal entities, communities as potential human resources and consumers, and governmental regulation as a strong and ultimate element of controlling corporate behavior in the context of specific legally and morally acceptable principles. Social issues cannot be underemphasized. Economic prosperity cannot be the one and only mission of a business. Furthermore, environmental protection is not the only important issue in terms of social responsibility. It is impossible to secure growth through implementing practices for the environment, while you have exhausted human resources providing them with unhealthy and unpleasant work conditions. Also, it is not possible to believe that social issues can be handled better through private initiatives and corporate programs alone than governmental intervention. Inevitably, corporations, government, and society must cooperatively work, develop an ethical system of common values, exploit resources more efficiently, and serve the interests of all parties involved by approaching a balance point between conflicting issues and interests.

Moreover, practitioners must consider the trends and insights of each era and make principles that can be changed when the beliefs or implementation methods evolve. This flexibility gives the opportunity to adopt changes more efficiently than retaining principles that are not aligned with new practices and needs. Either it is a major or a minor change that takes place due to the developments in the internal or external corporate environment; all individuals must be well informed about the change. Corporate policies must describe and explain why on an optimum level the change is important, what factors are critical to consider the change, and how the latter can be implemented through corporate practices and operations. The capability to change in favor of societal interest or governmental regulation can be a key element of success and competitive advantage. Corporations that cannot consider their responsibilities as legal entities are not capable of retaining market share or recording a sustainable path of growth. Issues regarding business ethics can generate substantial changes in corporate policies, and decision makers must take important steps toward the development of an ethical set of principles.

Ethical CSR Activities

Considering that CSR activities are very important for each organization, the main concept behind ethical CSR activities is to associate moral awareness with traditional and emerging social needs. Starting from the corporate workplace, rational corporate responsibility extends up to the general market, the community within which it operates, and the environment. Hence, corporations develop their virtue ethics as a normative theory of ethics that mentions an individual's character to be the primary subject of moral judgment. Thus, virtue, as a character and thought attribute that allows an individual to achieve the implementation of morals, is responsible for the development of corporate policies that influence moral behaviors within and outside the range of operations of an organization.

A corporation cannot be characterized as virtuous unless its people present a strong moral behavior and attitude. The critical role of the human factor is the protagonist of corporate policies, as the workforce from the entry level up to the top level is responsible for creating, developing, integrating, and reviewing corporate socially responsible behaviors. For instance, Aristotle argued that the virtues were acquired gradually by practice and laid down by long education, while by the time an individual reaches the middle age, it is very difficult to radically change his or her orientation. Thus, achieving responsible business practices through rational policies implemented by human resources can be done with strong internal communication and training programs, focusing on ethical awareness, while the corporation, as an entity, produces goods and services efficiently and serves the needs of consumers. "A complete ethic needs to be person-centered and act-focused, dynamic as well as static, developmental and decision-focused, and contextually adaptable" (Whetstone 2001, 112).

Limitless growth without considering cost and negative consequences to other entities, and the expectation that always there will be room for an increase in corporate revenue cannot suggest an ethical corporate policy. Organizations must raise their focus on fair and moral consumer treatment by providing products aligned with generally acceptable principles on health and safety. Additionally, the supply chain must be developed with moral policies, while corporations are responsible for ethical research and development. The community in which a corporation operates is significantly important, as if the society forms an unethical picture about a corporation, then its failure is inevitable in some cases. Hence, it is crucial to respect the society, its norms and expectations, its capabilities in terms of education and skills developed, such as the existence of skilled human resources trained by advanced educational institutions, and offer fair, transparent, and equal opportunities to people. Corporations, even if their activities are international, must support local communities with initiatives and moral activities associated with societal well-being and development characteristics.

Environmental issues are once again very important, particularly since the increased environment awareness of the recent decades, due to pollution, health, and climate change issues as they emerge. Global warming is about the rise in average global temperature due to the impact from forcing mechanisms such as concentration of greenhouse gases in the atmosphere and solar activity. Greenhouse gases, such as carbon dioxide, methane, and nitrous oxide, occur naturally in the atmosphere, but also as a result of human activities such as fossil fuel use, deforestation, waste of resources, and agriculture exploitation. This implies that corporate policies must develop climate adaption practices, aiming at managing rationally natural resources, protecting ecosystems, and adjusting activities in such a way to cope with the consequences of climate change.

Exploiting ethically natural resources is critical for each organization and being environmentally friendly must be a top-priority policy. Climatic variability has always been a condition of survival for species. Human beings are not an exception. Responding to climate change requires local, regional, national, and international responsibility in terms of actions. Policy makers must understand and analyze the social environment in which the corporation operates and identify the areas in which corporate activities might improve environmental value. Also, as climate and environment in general record an unprecedented pace of change, policy makers must consider the feedback of corporate activities, and develop strategies on how these could be more rational than previous implementations, achieving higher levels of environmental and corporate performance.

CSR activities must be measured and evaluated, considering their effectiveness toward the organization, human resources, and the environment in which they operate. For instance, following the Great Depression of 1929 and the subprime lending crisis in 2008, the governments and global institutions have increased the level of rules and law coverage over corporate practices. Consequently, organizations focus on environmental protection, on the development of a comprehensive code of conduct, on programs about health and safety, as well as on activities on charity and the general support of the community. Therefore, moral corporate policies cover environmental and economic issues, the responsibility of producing goods and services according to regulations and law, and most importantly the employee rights and labor practices in terms of the development of a sustainable work environment.

For instance, the International Organization for Standardization (ISO) has published a guide under the term of ISO 26000:2010 covering different aspects of social responsibility (ISO 2010). Implementing such framework can enhance the corporate competitive advantage, its reputation, and the ability to bolster its employees' morale and commitment, corporate productivity rates, and its relationship with consumers, suppliers, shareholders, governments, and community in which it operates.

Particularly, the principles of social responsibility include accountability, transparency, ethical behavior, and respect for stakeholder interests, the rule of law, international norms of behavior, and human rights. Therefore, recognizing the subject of social responsibility activities is crucial, as it affects the general organizational governance, in terms of work environment, labor practices, fair operating practices, and policies on the environment, employee involvement, and community.

Moreover, policy makers employ different approaches on how to conduct a set of guidelines in order to promote ethical CSR activities. Indeed, financial performance, labor relations, and the impact of corporate practices toward society have been always a challenging process for policy makers. Thus, the implementation of a rational package of policies eliminates any inconvenience in terms of being associated with unethical corporate practices. This suggests that the actions taken to ensure adherence to ethical corporate policies are very important for each sector and business industry.

Practitioners must not ignore and undermine human rights, while the product itself is similarly essential to consider. Corporate policies on product hazards and consumer complaints must be developed in such a way that respond to consumer demands and the society. It can be stated that corporation's willingness to take responsibility on a specific issue does not mean that people will accept that as a fact, in terms of ignoring the issue and its consequences. Undeniably, some corporations may take advantage of their size and volume of operations, particularly for multinational companies in order to make the community forget the unethical practices. However, a moral thinker cannot be satisfied with this policy. It is impossible to implement strategies of avoiding your responsibilities by exploiting other's vulnerability.

The effectiveness of CSR activities on decreasing or eliminating the level of unethical and unlawful conduct in an organization cannot be measured only with raw data and key indicators. Instead, the efficiency of implementing strategies and corporate policies that have ethics as their core procedure can be visualized as the creation of an ethical work climate. Though the societal culture as a very powerful factor that influences the behavior of individuals, the work environment can be even greater in terms of developing a strong relationship with individuals. Some employees may be more susceptible to the influence of corporate policies, while others may have solid sensitivity and cannot accept the change effortlessly. Therefore, there is no common procedure to identify the level of commitment on CSR programs, but at the same time, corporate policies can be a dominating factor for shaping new thoughts and perceptions for individuals and entire communities.

Hence, the epicenter of the establishment of such programs is the argument against illegal behavior. This is a priority for each corporation, as it has legal consequences not only to the individual who act illegally, but also to the organization that the practitioner represents toward the consumers, suppliers, shareholders, community, and government. Thus, regular ethical courses and in-depth analysis wherever individuals cannot directly realize the impact of their activities is very critical for a successful CSR program.

Loyalty toward the ethical principles and procedures of the corporation means that no one is authorized to act unethically, even if the behavior stems from a high-level executive. Individuals must follow an integral concept of behavior, in terms of acting morally because they want to, and not because they are forced to do it. With honesty and respect, corporate policies can develop individual mindset capacity in the context of ethics, and consequently create a healthy corporate environment in which individuals want to contribute the most, while they raise concerns for the other employees, the corporation as an entity, the environment, and the society in which they belong and operate.

Moral Employer Brand

Building an ethical corporation and employer brand signifies that corporate policies must develop a set of qualities, attributes, and ethical considerations that make the corporation an important and valuable part for society and responsible to all the other entities. The brand is the core component of a corporate's reputation, while there is a clear link between the latter and ethical branding (Fan 2005). Thus, it is important to analyze corporate goals, the procedures that are required to create an efficient and moral working environment, the capacity of opportunities that the organization can provide to local, regional, national, and international resources, and the terms and conditions of employment that it offers. Concerning the above conditions, corporate policies must create a moral brand image of the organization that the employees, shareholders, and society accept through the time. The brand is not only a status of reputation for a business. A moral employer has a series of benefits, such as claim of a larger marker share, attraction of best human resources, better negotiations with suppliers, and the creation of a multidimensional channel of partners and loyal consumers.

Creating a moral employer brand is not easy. Policy makers must analyze what society and human resources expect from the organization and consider their needs and wants in order to provide better opportunities. Undeniably, corporate climate and its core values can have a significant impact on individuals and their perceptions. Particularly, CSR initiatives and policies can shape employee perceptions and affect employee commitment and motivation (Collier and Esteban 2007). Hence, it is important to build an environment that enhances fairness and meritocracy, by providing human resources a trustworthy relationship of development and excellence. At the same time, these core values of the organization can have a strong impact on the society in which the corporation operates. Therefore, it is essential for each corporation to develop policies that promote human rights, environmental activities for the common good, and bolster people's potential to perform better and achieve personal goals.

Moral employer brand, as a concept of CSR and reputation management, is crucial for the development of business ethics. Indeed, there is a positive relationship between perceived CSR and reputation, as well as between employer brand perception and reputation (Verčič and Ćorić 2018). Practices employed by corporations aimed at improving the view of other entities, such as the public perception of a local or wider community, and the beliefs of consumers, employees, investors, and business partners. Communicative activities through extended marketing plans and events related to the public relations department of an organization cannot create a positive attitude toward the corporation unless the latter presents moral values.

Covering unethical practices by promoting positive reputational management is a process that can decrease the real value of a corporation. Reliability, trustworthiness, and validity are not perceptions that can be developed instantly, or just by implementing a great communicational strategy. For instance, in the context of trustworthiness, values such as honesty, integrity, transparency, loyalty, and the process of keeping promises are essential for the development of a moral individual, and consequently for the development of a moral employer brand. Loyalty from employees, consumers, community, and other interested parties can be developed only in a way that the corporation implements strategies of mutual respect, considering other entities as part of the core CSR program.

Business history shows that corporations can have a disastrous downturn if people do not recognize their unethical side on practices, such as providing consumers products and services that are harmful for their health or treat employees without considering their values and needs. Particularly in times of crises such as the 2008 financial crisis or the 2020 pandemic outbreak, corporations have seen an extended focus on active reputation management, even though at the same time, their employees may have psychological issues due to exhausting work conditions, while in some extreme cases the weakest employees may lead themselves even to suicide. This is a reality, and since the mass production becomes a common practice in the entrepreneurial world, and because of the ever-increasing competition in the global economy, some corporations completely ignore their core mission on values and ethics, putting financial performance as their only priority without considering the consequences of their practices to other entities and to the society in which they operate.

Therefore, the suggestion that corporations are ethically acceptable if they are legal can lead to wrong perceptions. Indeed, corporate policies must be rational and moral. This demonstrates that an effective strategy about moral employer brand development must include practices of fairness and meritocracy. The spectrum of such practices must be morally associated with each corporate operation. A good reputation that has its roots to unethical and misleading information is not acceptable. A moral thinker must recognize that the problem is not the possibility of the widespread of a scandal, but the scandal itself. We care what other individuals think about us, and this is a totally unintentional process. People tend to compare situations considering a wide range of different conditions and criteria, and then form perceptions about specific issues that they are interested at. Also, some corporations may believe that by staying silent about topics such as work climate and employee well-being or environmental care, they can avoid any bad reputation development. However, this practice cannot be evaluated as acceptable by a rational and ethical organization. Policy makers cannot ignore the reality, they must not put aside ethics for the best of the interests of some individuals or entities, and they should increase their moral capacity in the context of influencing other individuals to ethical behavior, on the level that they are capable of.

Building a corporate identity of ethics and making a company socially responsible require a set of flexible and solid core values based on the *moral entity consideration* principle. If a policy maker attempts to copy corporate policies of other brands, the result will not be as much as efficient as an original strategy. Additionally, common standards on corporate regulatory controlled by public authorities are essential to exist; however, this process cannot ensure a universal implementation of common policies because of rather different corporate characteristics and resources, thus whether a corporation is capable of adhering to these standards. When an organization proceeds with the announcement that its core policies are aligned with international standards over a specific concern, this does not necessarily mean that the corporate practices are entirely ethical.

A corporation must cope with unethical or even illegal behavior on the part of its employees or executives. Individuals have their own perspective on ethical dilemmas in the workplace or in their personal life. Thus, though policy makers are not authorized to control any aspect of individual's personal life, as people are responsible for their behavior in a community, corporate agents are responsible for the level of ethical awareness that the employees present within the context of work environment. This indicates that corporate policies must include a variety of activities for transferring and promoting moral thinking and practices to everyone in the workplace. In response to this, practitioners must formulate codes of conduct and communicate multidimensional moral guidelines, such as conducting internal ethical audits. Also, they must provide employees seminars and knowledge sessions on how to become a moral thinker, and how to behave ethically, not because they must due to corporate policies or social norms, but because it must be due an internal process as an attempt to be a valuable part of a community.

Concluding Remarks

Business ethics is interconnected to the dimensions of CSR, divided into the core and societal responsibilities of a corporation. The moral actions of the latter are directly associated with organizational sustainability, which entails to a broader range of obligations that corporations have toward society beyond maximizing their profits. Being ethical is a continuous and very demanding process. Practitioners need to prioritize corporate needs considering a variety of factors in the context of their internal and external environment. Policy makers must take actions that are aligned with law and ethical minimum, while given the available resources, human capital, and organizational size, corporate policies can be developed in such a valuable way to serve rationally both corporate mission and society expectations. This conveys how a moral employer brand can be formed, and how you can build loyalty, trust, integrity, and values, instead of covering unethical practices.

CHAPTER 4

Managing Ethical Behavior: Ethical Code

The presence of human activity in a corporation can be conceptualized as the quality and quantity of its behavior in the context of its contribution to the operations and outcomes. This is a complicated and very demanding process for human resources, based on behavioral science knowledge, while Jones (1991) highlighted that there is a negative link between moral intensity and attributions of responsibility. People think that their actions are less accountable, and they cannot understand the level of their responsibility. Therefore, the establishment of a code of ethics implies that members of a group such as an organization must comply with the code in order to remain part of the group. The need of a code of conduct is as necessary as in social life for development both in society and business (Lee 1926). The use of a code of ethics extends beyond professional environments, and it generates a crucial impact on the society in general.

Ethical principles and codes of conduct have never been evolved enough to prevent professionals from developing additional ways of handling ethical conduct of behaviors. Indeed, it is impossible to claim that in modern world business ethics cannot be evolved anymore, as they reached the limit of ethical consideration. In practice, while human capital evolves its mind capacity and ways of thinking, business ethics and morals in general are being developed as well. Various changes in moral values are becoming fundamentals in codes of conduct once they become essential for doing ethical business. Hence, it is critical to retain a development pace on moral principles in order to consider the behaviors and needs of each era and its societal characteristics. For instance, Schwartz (2002) indicates a set of six moral standards including trustworthiness, respect, responsibility, fairness, caring, and citizenship as a guide to construct a code of ethics by which corporations can be ethically audited for compliance.

Burton and Goldsby (2009, 146) claimed that "an action can be morally obligatory, morally forbidden, or morally permissible." Obligatory actions are those that are morally right to do, and wrong not to do, while morally forbidden actions are those that are wrong to do and right not to do. Morally neutral actions, such as permissible actions, are those where any option in a situation will not violate the moral standard. In order to challenge with the above conditions, organizations have a written code called a code of ethics that governs standards of professional conduct expected during corporate governance and employment relations. This ethical code is meant to provide guidelines and fundamental principles for desired behavior by human resources in a corporation. Though it is impossible to guarantee the implementation of the code of conduct, the existence of this element does not mean that an organization is ethical and morally acceptable by its internal and external parties of interest. Either the ethical code consists of just one paragraph or multiple pages, the fact that it exists cannot retain a moral profile for the corporation.

As a sum of rules and procedures that specifies what each human in a business should and should not do in rather different situations, a code of ethics cannot predict future challenges, such as advanced technology integration. Thus, codes in themselves are inadequate in addressing complex ethical issues generated by interest conflicting and the rather different perceptions and values of individuals. Furthermore, even if most employees perceive the code of conduct, one individual is usually enough to break this chain of moral culture and cause a series of conflicts. Therefore, corporate policies must be well developed and designed in order to be implemented fairly and equally by all members. This implies that members of an ethical organization must respect corporate policies, work relationships, diversity, confidentiality and privacy, internal and external law environment and requirements, and be honest with each other. Demonstration of commitment to a professional level is a constant challenge, and practitioners must not have the authority to exploit other individuals and their needs.

Professional behavior is governed by the moral principles and values of the corporation, which may or may not be embedded in a code of ethics. *Moral entity consideration* must be a prioritized principle for people in corporations and business practice. This indicates that businesspeople must consider the rights of other individuals; the principles of social and natural justice; and the need to achieve equity, meritocracy, fairness, and consistency in managing behaviors. Employment decisions can be very difficult. However, practitioners must increase their moral capacity at the level at which they can adopt flexible policies and implement the code of conduct on each occasion. As explained in a previous chapter, moral thinking is crucial to influence individuals behave ethically. Professionalism in the corporate world means acting in accordance with ethical standards and principles, which governs how people should behave in formal or even informal situations.

Therefore, organizational ethical codes provide policies, procedures, guidelines, and rules on what is a moral behavior. This set of principles is expressed in a code of business ethics, which is also called code of business conduct. It is both a general and specific reference point in terms of how to be moral and act ethically. Thus, it includes details about organizational ethical values and standards, promotes commitment, describes the critical path as a guidance of how this can be achieved through fair corporate policies, and identifies additional supporting rules that enable the implementation of business ethics, such as a harassment policy, a bullying policy, an employee voice policy, or a behavioral reward policy.

The main purpose of a code of conduct is to embed a set of ethical values into organizational procedures, strategies, and practices by supporting ethical behavior providing guidance on how to make moral decisions that are compatible with the organization's ethical standards. Hence, ethical codes can be considered within the context of an organization's culture (McNutt and Batho 2005), as it shapes a corporate climate of integrity and fairness to facilitate a sustainable business. The existence of a strong ethical code can minimize risks in terms of consistency and enhance trust levels among people, as well as their contribution at an organizational, social, economic, and environmental level.

Though it is not possible to have a universal morally neutral definition of a moral problem as it depends on various approaches (Morris 2004), the code of ethics as part of corporate policies must be straightforward, clear, transparent, and must promote integrity. It can be divided into parts, chapters, articles, and paragraphs, such as the scope of code of conduct, professional behavior and competence, corporate ethical standards and principles, a declaration of interests, procedure for conflicts of interest, moral collegiality and discretion, principles regarding individual and corporate integrity, transparency policies, and the application of the code (Table 4.1). For instance, it can mention that you should, as an employee and member of the organization, base resourcing, training, development, evaluation, promotion, and termination decisions on qualifications, performance, and business considerations, or make it clear to not discriminate other people according to sex, gender, race, age, marital status, and ethnic origin. It can provide individuals with warnings about harassment, abuse, or lack of respect and consideration as unacceptable

Table 4.1   Code of ethics statement

Code of Conduct
Article 1: Scope This Code of Conduct shall apply to the employees of the corporation.
Article 2: Principles • Put loyalty and fairness to the highest moral principles. • Be honest and respect other individuals and entities. • Conduct business in compliance with law. • Comply with safety, health, and security regulations. • Do not make discrimination and immediately expose such incidents. • Follow directives of supervisors. • Provide products and services of the highest quality.
Article 3: Procedure for Conflicts of Interest • Avoid any situation that may give rise to a conflict of interest between two or more individuals and/or entities. • Comply with regulation regarding financial interests. • Pay for unlawful purposes and bribe are prohibited. • Expose corruption as soon as you become aware of it. • Do not propagate false or misleading information. • Corporate authorities shall take any measure they consider appropriate in the light of the information referred. • Employees are personally accountable for their duties.
Article 4: Application of the Code Corporate authorities shall ensure proper application of this Code of Conduct. Employees shall inform authorities in a timely manner if they have doubts regarding the application of this Code before acting on the matter relating to which the doubts arise.

behaviors that are not tolerated in the workplace, promote rules fostering an ethical, loyal, fair, and healthy working environment, with respect on the dignity of the individual, and mention that employees shall dress in business attire.

Moreover, it can include a statement in order to seek development and employ more efficient and economical methods for getting tasks accomplished. Also, it can distinguish personal from corporate benefit by mentioning that employees must not use corporate property and resources for personal benefit. Similarly, the code of ethics should include rules to maintain confidentiality of records and clearly not use any information coming to employees confidentially as a means for making private profit. Finally, it must be noted as a core rule to behave and perform your duties as an employee with independence, integrity, discretion in compliance with corporate rules, while everyone must perform assigned duties to the best of their capabilities.

In any case, the development of a code of ethics is not limited to certain rules and guidelines, thus policy makers can conduct the code of ethics that is most suitable to the corporate mission and goals. Furthermore, implementing an international ethical code is quite challenging, particularly for multinational corporations dealing with international markets, cultures, and globalized competition. Indeed, the code of ethics should be based on simple, universal values (Smeltzer and Jennings 1998); however, this is not possible due to a plethora of conditions. Schwartz (2005) stated that the identification of universal moral values is a necessary but insufficient step in the process of establishing a code of ethics, leaving many practical issues unanswered. For instance, values such as respect, responsibility, and fairness can be interpreted differently. At the same time, a code of ethics is often insufficient in the context of rather different business conditions and challenges. We must recognize that a universal code could only exist if it includes flexible general principles on fundamental moral guidelines that must be translated and modified into corporate needs.

Over and above, the code of conduct must have a spiritual sense, in the name of developing core values and principles that are specific enough to influence employees and show them how they are supposed to behave as members of the entity. People cannot apply the code of ethics easily, as it is a process that has many dimensions. Particularly, business ethics principles usually illustrate a narrow set of issues, as an attempt to cover main core values, instead of moral obligations on each business segment and operation. It is almost impossible to address each aspect of business ethics. Thus, it is recommended to give guidance and directions based on *moral entity consideration*. In other terms, the code of conduct supported training of individuals to increase their moral thinking capacity and embedded corporate culture within their daily behavior.

Since there is no universally agreed ethical framework on how to behave morally, different situations require personal evaluation of the individual. The latter's decision and judgment involve choices that may have a strong impact on other entities. Hence, moral judgment as a process of thinking is concerned with attitudes and personal insights, instead of common rules and practices. In light of this, corporations must develop a more complete ethical policy, while policy makers and businesspeople should be characterized as moral practitioners. Particularly, in order to qualify as a moral person, to be a moral agent, an entity must be capable of genuine rational intentional (or voluntary) actions (French 2015). Hence, it is essential to increase moral awareness at a level of which an entity is no more following internal interest, but is driven by common ethical norms.

Corporate policies are named to cope with this challenge by introducing a set of values that are commonly acceptable and feasible to achieve. These policies are regularly influenced by various theories, such as the deontological theory, the stakeholder theory, or utilitarianism. Starting with the deontological theory, the morality of a behavior should be based on a series of predefined rules with respect to other entities, rather than on the consequences of the action. This theory is commonly contrasted with consequentialism, as a class of normative ethical theories that considers the consequences of an individual's conduct. This suggests that a morally right behavior will produce a morally acceptable outcome.

Deontological ethics highlights the rightness or wrongness of an individual's conduct. Particularly, the deontological decision theory develops a set of both necessary and sufficient conditions being permissible given an agent's imperfect information (Lazar 2017). However, the stakeholder theory states that the corporation should be managed according to its stakeholders' rules, such as its owners, employees, consumers, suppliers, and the society in which it operates. Though this theory can achieve long-term growth and prosperity, in practice there are many corporations that on behalf of their profits and interests, they modify the corporate policies. Indeed, there are many cases where conflicting interests between different entities make it difficult to decide who to believe, and whose behavior is more moral than others. Consequently, the interests of stakeholders are being prioritized against other entities, as it is very difficult to achieve a balance between ethics and financial returns, in a globalized and competitive business environment. Hence, trust and cooperation are key elements of the stakeholder theory in order to have a competitive advantage (Jones 1995). The pressure to achieve financial results, provide normal prices, support employees with benefits, and make goods and services that are ethically produced, promoted, and consumed, involves contraventions between corporate owners, employees, suppliers, consumers, and society.

Therefore, resolving ethical dilemmas is not an easy task, as individuals are limited to their capability in terms of understanding the conditions of a situation and how to behave morally and rationally. Also, it is worth noting that many business leaders will not sacrifice their moral awareness to secure a financial gain, making them the perfect example of how a moral leader must be. In some occasions, agents must take actions that might be unethical, though they maximize value; while in other circumstances, they must take actions that do not optimize resources but are ethically required and mandated. Thus, sometimes agents and in general businesspeople, whether they are employees, shareholders, or suppliers, have conflicting responsibilities and must decide what to do, and how to do it ethically.

Additionally, in some cases, individuals can get addicted to unethical action, as the exemption from being punished by authorities, or in other words, the freedom from the nonpenalized consequences of action, which is closely related to the notion of autonomy. This is an indication that those individuals feel powerful by serving interests with means that are against or even harmful to other entities. Therefore, impunity is not only unethical, but it consists of a wrong example to other individuals by not responding to these behaviors. Corporate policies based on the harmfulness of other entities are unacceptable even if they exploit legal interpretations or other unregulated practices. The consequence of violation of the code of ethics is a disciplinary process applied by corporate policies and government law, and it must be clear, fair, and strict, depending on each case. Hence, the existence of a solid ethical code means that individuals are required to be guided not only by their self-interests and their personal expectations, or the interests of the organization they work for, but also by the wider good of society in which they operate and live in. We all have ethical responsibilities to other entities and our behavior must be aligned to fundamental ethical obligations by applying the primary principle of *moral entity consideration*.

At this point, we meet utilitarianism as the belief that a behavior resulting in maximizing the production of goodness, happiness, and the well-being for most of the population is moral. "Utilitarianism may lead to the moral justification of the prevalence of profit-making and economic value maximization" (Renouard 2011, 87), while this theory belongs to the consequentialist ethical theories, which considers the result of behaviors and the equality between different entities, claiming that the best outcome is the one in which utility is maximized. However, it is noticeable that the ethical concepts of equity and justice are just the medium to apply business ethics. Managing ethical behavior means that people must be influenced by these theories, understand them to the best of their mental capabilities, evaluate their values, and then try to apply these fundamentals to their actions with fairness and meritocracy against other entities.

Finally, it is important to cultivate one additional approach regarding the development of an ethical image, in order to avoid regulation. The existence of a code of conduct can enhance corporate reputation and discourage government intervention, as an attempt for organizations to manage themselves with less regulation (Stevens and Buechler 2013). This highlights that corporations can exploit legal methods in terms of achieving a balanced moral reputation and make authorities believe that they have an enhanced and multilevel code of conduct that is well applied, in order to decrease the volume of authoritative control over corporate operations and the level of regulations required to implement. For instance, corporate policies can include a series of values and ethical norms as a comprehensive guide for employees, but at the same time the management can implement unethical practices in the name of their position, and consequently workforce will follow. In some cases, if an individual or a group of individuals reacts to this practice, they may be threatened with layoffs, so exposing such practices is difficult to achieve.

Moral Organizational Design

Organizational design, as the process of structuring corporate operations in a functional and rational system for maximizing means and resource utility, is a critical procedure for each corporation. Moral organizational design requires additional notions of ethical consideration in the context of defining morally acceptable job roles, ethical activity and responsibility distribution, and flexible procedures about achieving organizational and individual goals by morally exploiting people skills, infrastructure, and capital. Policy makers must recognize that the strategic principles of the organization should embrace the needs and rights of employees as well as those of the corporation.

While organizations evolve in conjunction with the progress of its people that operate the business functions, as well as the developments of the environment in which the organization operates, this is a complicated process that requires multidimensional approaches. Overall, the main aim of corporate design is to exploit as rational as possible all the available resources of people, infrastructure, and capital, in order to achieve organizational strategic goals. After clarification of the purposes of the organization, the next step is to define as precisely as possible the activities that are required to achieve efficiency, and then distribute them to individuals based on their skills, needs, and expectations. It is important to mention that there is not one best organizational design, as there are as many alternatives as policy makers. There is always a choice, which can be more effective than the alternatives.

Certainly, developing and managing behaviors is quite a demanding process. There is an ongoing relationship between corporate strategies and the environmental changes in which it operates. Furthermore, ethics reflect the transformations of both internal and external environment of the corporation. Internal factors, such as changes in working arrangements and the availability of skills, the development of new activities or services, the potential performance downturn or growth, and a poor or great work climate, could create a combination of elements that can lead the organizational design to failure or success. Additionally, external factors that are likely to affect the organization design, such as political, economic, social, technological, legal, and environmental issues, are also very important for the sustainability of an organization and the implementation of business ethics. Thus, redesign of an organization is critical, as it can lead to long-term wealth creation for the benefit of employees, communities, the environment, and investors (Kelly and White 2009). Corporations and individuals are not static entities, and they evolve their behaviors constantly. Hence, corporate structures and policies are strongly influenced by individual and societal perceptions, alongside their strengths and weaknesses.

Most individuals are driven by internal forces for personal growth and development. This signifies that they need to be part of a moral, supportive, challenging, and well-optimized organizational environment. Moreover, moral organizational design must be settled in the sense of human satisfaction, as the dynamics that arise on the level of employment relationships can have a major effect on the behavior of the members of a corporation. The implementation of such strategies must include actions that are human-centered. This implies that the systematic data gathering from people about rather different operational or other kind of issue must not ignore business ethics and its importance.

Data are the number one factor of a successful and moral organizational design. Data management is one of the most essential elements for organizational performance. But data alone cannot provide any solutions. Also, you cannot treat people as data sources. For instance, some individuals may accept working in a position even if it is not under their preferences. This means that when you conduct a survey to gather data from your employees, you may have feedback material that is not in accordance with the real conditions. In many cases, an attitude test cannot identify the well-hidden perceptions, needs, commitment level, and feelings of an individual. That is why agents must be very close to their human workforce because data technical scientists and machine intelligence cannot cover and consider all the aspects of a human entity.

Consequently, *moral entity consideration*, as the primary principle of this book, suggests that organizational design includes both the exploitation of valid data and information and understanding capabilities of human resources, considering business ethics. The strategic plan must not only be quick, flexible, valid, and effective, but it must integrate ethics in its core elements, in order to motivate people, raise adaptability, and gain commitment to achieve increased performance and levels of well-being.

Individual Well-Being

The well-being of an individual, or in other words the welfare of human resources, can be presented by various approaches. All employees are willing to receive support by the corporation they are working for, in order to contribute with most of their capabilities in the long term. This can have a strong positive impact on the business, as the increase in motivation level reduces work climate concerns and conflicts between individuals. Particularly, perceived employee development practices can lead to lower levels of work effort among employees (Nerstad, et al. 2018). However, there is no ultimate and universal guide on how to manage to create an environment of fairness and growth as people are rather different, so they form each work environment independently, though there are some policies that could be part of an initial approach on how to develop such a practice in the context of rational corporate policies.

It is vital to begin with the basics. Having clean living and healthy work conditions is the fundamental key for human satisfaction in terms of their basic needs. Although this statement could be presented as an unnecessary remark for many practitioners, in fact there are many corporations that do not implement and communicate such policies about the work conditions that individuals must work into. This is crucial, as well as the existence of policies that offer a shelter for personal stuff or even a personal desk, and healthy meals where it is possible to provide. For instance, due to the development of flexible work relationships, many workers are on the go almost the entirety of their daily working hours, while others practice remote working and they are at their home. So, corporations must have policies that enhance daily healthy meals programs, clean working conditions, provide packages in the context of health insurance such as annual health check to prevent illness and reduce absenteeism, and support of personal life in terms of work–life balance or other benefits for the families of the employees, in order to increase the levels of loyalty and commitment, and their well-being in general.

It is essential to reduce the level of stress and anxiety in the corporate environment, and increase overall satisfaction, motivation, and productivity levels. For instance, some individuals cannot be productive in the early hours of the days or others may want to support their family activities and demands such as during childbirth, so a flexible arrival time within a rational period such as within 30 minutes, while lengthening similarly the departure time of those employees, or fair paternity leaving programs, could be beneficial for both individuals and the organization. Additionally, for those working remotely, this does not mean that they are free of duties, thus they must be professional and balance their home conditions in the context of working and personal life. Fast-paced cities and life trends promote a life of mobility and demanding challenges. Therefore, it is very important for a worker to feel that their supervisors, and even their coworkers, will understand from a moral standpoint why they need some indulgence on their behavior.

Over the above example of someone who must support his or her family, a single individual may claim that it is not fair to have flexible policies, as it could consist of discrimination. However, this behavior must be protected by corporate policies, as the rationale of such practices relies on individual well-being and not on discrimination between employees. Thus, it would not be fair to offer additional break time to some employees or accept reduction in the quantity of work hours of some individuals only. But it would be morally acceptable to support all employees in the name of well-being, as this process can reduce conflicts and enhance both worker morale and corporate image in the broader community.

Additionally, corporate initiatives such as organizing meetings for employees and their families, or the establishment and support of annual reward events in order to recognize employee contribution in practice are methods that can improve the satisfaction and well-being of employees. All workers need to feel that their contribution is valued and well appreciated by the corporation and their coworkers. This process develops employee collaboration, and individuals are seeking to offer more in terms of accepting interesting challenges, instead of demanding more for less contribution. People must not feel afraid of informal communication. It is not healthy to apply strict policies that lead individuals to feel uncomfortable and exhausted of remembering a set of rules, else they could be fired. On the contrary, bearing in mind a *moral entity consideration* approach, individuals can enjoy being part of a team and a corporation with values and principles, thus they could increase their efficiency rates and achieve both personal and organizational goals.

For instance, recognition programs and events are critical in the name of the social media age. This indicates that people tend to upload on the Internet their routine, their daily contribution to a variety of concepts, such as achievements at work or at home, new educational certificates and qualifications, the places that they feel happy and have fun such as being at a club or at a sports stadium, and their thoughts about rather different topics and trends. Moreover, they share on their profile pages on various online platforms a series of personal times, such as a birthday party, or taking vacations to a great place that everyone would be jealous of. Sharing information with others is a way of receiving recognition and feeling more valuable in terms of scaling satisfaction through various rating systems. The latter can be expressed by feedback evaluation mechanisms such as trophies and awards of completion or participation in an event and ceremonies, certificates, special bonuses, and other forms of recognition of contribution translated into monetary packages or other benefits, which are directly associated with the well-being of an individual.

The concept of being motivated through recognition consists of a multidimensional approach in terms of evolutionary biology and other critical factors such as economic conditions. Lawrence (2010, 69) argued that "if morality is a skill set devised to coordinate two innate, unconscious, and potentially conflicting drives, it is rooted in emotions rather than cognitive principles," as there is an emerging behavioral query on how it is possible to acquire, defend, bond, and comprehend as a four-drive moral code without violating one's own drives. Therefore, corporate policies cannot prevent individuals from serving their own best interests, but they can promote a series of important actions that enhance fairness and ethics as principal moral drives of individual behavior. Ensuring the well-being of human resources is a complicated and timeless process. According to

the humanistic management theory and the humanistic model, the ultimate purpose of human existence is the notion of flourishing and well-
being (Pirson and Bachani 2018). Humans operate according to routines,
yet learn and adapt constantly, while dignity and morality are crucial to
achieve a level of well-being (Pirson 2017).

Hence, corporate policies must be updated with most recent employment regulation and labor law, and this should be documented as an
employee handbook in order to implement such practices. Policies must
focus on occupational health and safety, hygiene and sanitation programs,
promote fair rewards and recognition on employee behavior, and distribute job roles, tasks, and benefits equally in terms of meritocracy, and offer
opportunities as well as room for self-development. Also, everyone must
know what are the activities that they must do in the context of their job
with clear objectives, what behaviors are morally acceptable in terms of
business ethics and ensure that everyone is well informed on corporate
procedures.

At this point, it is important to mention the difference between
policies and guidelines. The latter term refers to corporate statements as
nonmandatory guides, while corporate policies consists of a series of documented elements that are crucial for the optimization of organizational
resources, and that without them the corporation could not achieve its
goals. Both policies and guidelines are important, but policies must be
implemented, while guidelines are partly compulsory, depending on a
variety of factors. For instance, if a worker can find new methods and
practices that could be more efficient than corporate guidelines, then this
could support the well-being of both the individual and the corporation,
so it is acceptable.

On the contrary, though policies must be flexible enough to adapt to
new trends, they must be at the same time rigorous in terms of controlling unexpected behavior that could lead to disastrous consequences. So,
if an individual violates corporate policies, then the reaction of corporate
authorities is way more significant in comparison with a potential violation of guidelines that are not considered as mandatory. The distinction
between these two categories is very important, as conflicting interests
usually end up with two or more individuals who claim corporate policies
or other formal and informal rules of conduct, in terms of supporting

their behavior. Hence, corporate policies must be rational enough to avoid such circumstances where individual well-being cannot be protected by regulations and other forms of frameworks for consistency and fairness.

In any case, corporate policies and guidelines are essential as a reference point for most issues emerging in an organization. This demonstrates that individuals can rely on written standards and defined boundaries that enable employees to understand clearly what is recommended to do, what is mandatory to apply as a process, what are the responsibilities, and what are the consequences of not being loyal on corporate policies. Handling conflicts is a demanding challenge, particularly if there is no reference framework that could be communicated between employees in order to be influenced and implement common practices through rational behavior and ensure professionalism.

Corporate Policy Framework

There is a plethora of corporate policy frameworks similar to the number of different characteristics that each company presents. Corporate policies, guidelines, and regulations reflect the core values of an organization's authorities, as policy makers are responsible for deciding which practices are most suitable for achieving organizational goals, and how resources should be influenced (human resources) or exploited (infrastructure) in the context of creating a work climate of growth and implement business ethics. Therefore, the process of developing a rational framework with moral corporate policies is vital for the sustainability of an organization.

A moral policy framework should start with fair administration regulations regarding attendance and leave alongside with time records management, regular work time, as well as individual work time regulations including a set of policies about overtime, part-time employment, seasonal, and other flexible employment relationships. Also, it must contain regulations and specialized conditions regarding a variety of employment issues such as sick leave, maternity and paternity leave, unpaid leave, and vacation. Payroll regulations are critical in order to implement ethical policies as well as providing fair compensation benefits to all workers depending on their contribution levels. Additionally, it is important to develop regulations about the health of employees, such as the hygiene in workplace, rules for cleaning and promote healthy actions in terms of eating and drinking during the workday; for instance, create a healthy place where you can have a meal, and other policies such as individual appearance and business attire, or strict rules on critical issues regarding smoking, alcohol, and drugs or medicine.

Furthermore, corporate policies must be understandable to everyone, so individuals can behave and develop their skills considering an ethical approach on their communication style, at either an internal or external standpoint. Communication is crucial for developing a moral brand and an ethical work environment, thus there must be regulations on distinguishing personal from business communicational style, and promote guidelines on how to professionally communicate through face-to-face discussions, the phone, text messages such as e-mails, and the use of personal devices in the work environment. Moreover, it is crucial to develop ethical principles in terms of confidentiality, as the management of important information is a very demanding challenge. Engagements outside the corporation should not trigger conflicts and have a negative impact on corporate culture, while individuals should not be allowed to create conflicts with other individuals, in terms of interpersonal differences. This is the reason why corporate policies must be comprehensive and completely fair regarding remuneration regulation, including job positioning, responsibility analysis, compensation packages, insurance coverage, and rules on contract termination. Likewise, the framework must include fair policies on performance evaluation, training needs and opportunities for self-development, internal transfers and promotions, employee assistance, and counseling.

Hence, corporate policies consist of a framework of useful and essential guidelines on a corporate level and shall be adapted by everyone involved in business operations. At the same time, it is necessary to implement practices that are aligned with legislation, cultural fit, and organizational needs and goals. This set of regulation includes the philosophy and values of the corporation and the vision of its owners and policy makers, the mission and organizational goals, the code of ethics as a vital part to success, a corporate social responsibility framework, and finally a set of policies regarding employee engagement, commitment, and involvement in the organization. Practitioners must evaluate the above criteria, so they are capable of investigating whether they encourage ethical behavior and reflect the organization's ethical values (Bonn and Fisher 2005), while it is very important to increase organizational information flow and communicate corporate policies and procedures to employees with much more effort (Hargie and Dickson 2007).

Though conducting an ethical corporate policy framework is a quite demanding process, by the time it is developed the corporation should immediately increase its values in terms of establishing a work environment with an underlined foundation for strategic organizational development and sustainability. Policy makers must conduct extensive research and ensure that policies are aligned with legal requirements, while they must involve experts of the field in order to create a framework that is timeless, precise, and fair for individuals. It is crucial to update corporate policies regularly and communicate to human resources through internal communicational corporate channels. Furthermore, it is essential to not overregulate, as this process can confuse individuals from understanding corporate policies and make it impossible to adhere.

Finally, it is critical to consider individuals as part of corporate policies and offer them the opportunity to get involved in the process of policy development, as this could be more efficient than attempting to control everyone and anything in the name of strict productivity. Hence, during the process of conducting and implementing an ethical corporate policy framework, individuals should feel that there is an increased level of fairness and meritocracy, with transparent, rational, and utilized policies that enable their capabilities. At the same time, there must not be any exceptions to cases of policy violation, as intolerable practices and unethical actions should be treated fairly for everyone.

Concluding Remarks

The presence of human activity in a corporation can be conceptualized as the amount of quality and quantity of its behavior in the context of its contribution to the operations. The establishment of a comprehensive code of ethics implies that members of a group such as an organization must comply with in order to remain part of the group. Handling ethical conduct of behaviors is a very challenging process, such as a demonstration of commitment to a professional level. The existence of a strong ethical code can minimize risks in terms of consistency and enhance trust levels among people. Accordingly, the main aim of corporate design is to exploit as rational as possible all the available resources of people, infrastructure, and capital, in order to achieve organizational strategic goals, while the importance of individual well-being is significant. All workers need to feel that their contribution is valued and well appreciated by the corporation and their coworkers. Finally, corporate policies and guidelines are essential as a reference point for most issues emerging in an organization.

CHAPTER 5

Agency Theory: Leadership and Management

The process of establishing an ethical corporation requires a moral attitude. The people engaged in the decision-making process, even if they are not responsible for the implementation of these actions, must consider moral values each time they make a policy and implement a decision. Agency theory relies on this chain of actions and responsibility. It addresses the relationship where in a contract "one or more persons (the principal(s)) engage another person (the agent) to perform some service on their behalf which involves delegating some decision making authority to the agent" (Jensen and Meckling 1976, 308). Under this circumstance, the principal and the agent are constantly in competition in terms of their personal moral attributes, while in case that the latter are not aligned with each other's beliefs it is not clear whose ethical code will be finally embedded in corporate policies.

Indeed, corporation history across various times and conditions has shown that agency theory is both important for the entities involved and critical for corporation sustainability. The issues associated with agency theory in corporations are almost limitless, due to conflict in maximizing interest, because the principal and the agent may have different values and principles. If their interests are not identical, then the process of moral prevalence between two or more parties is both crucial and vital for the corporation itself, as well as the society in which they operate. Hence, "agency theory reminds us that much of organizational life, whether we like it or not, is based on self-interest" (Eisenhardt 1989, 64).

In particular, the separation of ownership and control of the final actions, as the shareholders of a corporation or the board of directors can employ agents to run the business, as mentioned in a previous chapter, means that corporate owners can formulate a business code of ethics, but they cannot enforce it on the workforce unless the middle level of management is in coordination with their superiors. Thus, corporate holders are responsible for monitoring the performance of their agents to ensure that they act in the interest of the corporation, while they also need to retain and develop a social set of responsible and trustworthy policies.

Transfer of decision-making authority to agents and other individuals is important for any corporation. The capital demands of a business plan can be reached more easily if many investors contribute small portions to a large investment, thus creating a corporation. For this reason, investors employ agents to implement their vision of the corporate plan, because in some cases the cost of concentrating power in the hands of the shareholders could be too costly and inefficient for their expectations, while decreasing the objectivity in management of the corporation. Each party of an organization has its own responsibilities; hence, policies can be associated with different individuals, and this can lead to better moral efficiency as well. Aligning the interests of the agents with those of the shareholders is difficult to achieve, and may lead to unethical practices if the latter have strict policies and aims, such as maximizing value and returns, ignoring other implications and cost.

Consequently, it is very important for agents to be capable of making changes in their plans and policies, as the corporate world is an ever-changing globalized environment that can lead an organization to success or failure. There is no single fundamental procedure for making changes. There are many categories of change, such as the strategic, the operational, and the transformational; however, there is no guarantee that a single practice can end in change efficiency. Specifically, the median success rate of different types of change, such as strategy deployment, restructuring and downsizing, technology change, mixed set of change efforts, total quality management (TQM)-driven change, mergers and acquisitions, reengineering and process design, software development and installation, business expansion, and culture change, ranges from 19 percent to 58 percent, but these study results are not necessarily applicable to each situation (Smith 2002), because organizations are complex things and always change (Glenn and Malott 2004). Thus, each practitioner must understand the needs of the corporation and prepare multidimensional policies for upcoming challenges and unprecedented conditions.

Strategic change is about broad and long-term issues involving change. It needs a clear vision, aimed at growth, innovation, future-proof guidelines, quality, and advanced values concerning people. This type of change exploits various business resources such as finance, infrastructure, business culture, and human capital, within the context of the internal and external environment. Operational change is about creating new systems and procedures that can have a major and immediate effect on work conditions and thereby achieve increased efficiency. This direct approach is advantageous compared with strategic change in terms of the time it requires to produce a positive impact on corporate performance; however, this fast-paced change may be harmful for people and organizational culture. Also, transformational change is achieved through fundamental and structural changes in a corporation. Again, this can have a major effect on operational ways of current performance; yet it is useful in the context of making comprehensive changes and creating the basis for a new start and better corporate policies.

Hence, the feasibility of a corporate change starts with an advanced plan and analysis of the current situation, the position at which the corporation must be after the changes, and a comprehensive guide to how the change can be achieved without negatively impacting human resources and the organizational operations, and how it can reduce the effects of resistance to change, the possibility of low stability after change, as well as the possibility of a major loss in the context of corporate and people consistency. If you try to change people's behavior by implementing an aggressive approach, it is most probable that they will not be influenced, and thus the plan will be disastrous, as well as time consuming and costly for the corporation.

You cannot change perceptions of people and operational tasks instantly. They need to understand the need for the change, how it can be helpful for business efficiency, when it will have to be fully integrated in order to have a positive impact on business needs, and how they can contribute to this plan. Only then can their response to change be better and more efficient, giving them an internal feeling of responsibility for achieving the new goals of the organization. The change must have elements for each type of change previously mentioned, because the plan must have a long-term vision and innovative approaches, the capacity to produce a competitive advantage as soon as possible, and structural changes in terms of introducing new ways of creating value and making a sustainable business plan. In any case, the transition period is crucial for a corporation, and agents have increased responsibilities because they must incorporate both shareholders' expectations and human resource needs into a single business strategy. The latter must be analytical, rational, and ethical in order to convince people that the new plan is feasible and provide step-by-step guidelines for those that are conservative to change and an influential design for those who want to build trust and not compromise with past corporate conditions.

With this level of revitalization, and the spread of common aims and expectations to all individuals and entities of a corporate system, business ethics can be rationally integrated into policies and structures. Agents can create new opportunities with positive changes, and through rational decisions they can eliminate threats such as job insecurity, uncertainty, economic downsizing, or employee inconvenience. Therefore, it is very important for human resources to be part of the change and not followers of decisions from supervisors. This process is morally acceptable, because sustainable change requires strong commitment, trust, and a business culture of fairness, recognition, and human-oriented values.

Moral Leadership and Management

The characteristics of leadership and management have been associated with a wide range of important outcomes, such as productivity ratio, discipline level in a corporation, and people management. Leaders and managers play a concrete role in influencing the moral awareness and ethical behavior of labor in corporations. Their role can be proactive, reactive, or a mixture of both. They present characteristics that have a solid impact on employees' behavior, and therefore on the overall business consistency. The direct and indirect consequences of their policies on the organization and society are also critical. Their style affects the employees who work under their supervision and, consequently, the overall ethical behavior of the corporation.

Business ethics can be divided into two types: micro and macro (Brummer 1985). The micro type of ethics relies primarily on subordinates in an organization and concerns the internal processes, whereas the macro dimension arises principally for superiors and concerns the setting of corporate policies in general. Agents take decisions that affect mainly the macro environment of a corporation, whereas employees take decisions on the micro level, having relatively smaller consequences on business procedures. This distinction between micro and macro ethics is analogous to micro- and macroeconomic factors, and hence the macroenvironment deals with challenges of a broader economic and social policy than the microenvironment, which is concerned with economic and other sorts of decisions that an individual must take. It is important to mention that macro aspects affect micro issues and vice versa.

Leaders and managers must cope with microethical issues on a regular basis, and this is a very demanding process. The quality of their behavior is crucial for corporation development, and their control over ethical reasoning can be easily confused by external or internal factors. The moral capacity of policy makers shows their level of ethical qualities that are responsible for corporate moral awareness. Beyond the factors of individual interests and perspectives, the gravity of making moral corporate policies requires a strong ethical attitude at all levels of communication and behavior. Thus, defining leadership and management is very difficult, because the line between these two terms is blurred, and almost anyone can generate his or her own definition and approaches.

This is the reason why exploring the differences between leadership and management styles of corporate governance is critical. A corporation could be described as a complicated system of people value, infrastructure, technology, capital, and human resource hierarchy, where its processes from the very first action through the last behavior must be run smoothly and efficiently. Therefore, leadership and management include a variety of roles and corporate tasks, such as strategic planning, organizing, controlling, budgeting, problem solving, aligning the right people to the right job roles, implementing the ethical code, evaluating and promoting knowledge, moral sharing and storing of various types of information, offering rewards in the context of meritocracy, and achieving organizational goals on both a financial and social level.

For instance, leadership style can be indicated as coercive (demands compliance), authoritative (mobilizes people toward a vision), affiliative (creates harmony and emotional bonds), democratic (forges consensus), pacesetting (sets high standards), and coaching (develops people for the future) (Goleman 2000). Coercive and pacesetting leadership styles have an overall negative impact on work climate; affiliative, democratic, and coaching styles have a positive impact; and an authoritative style has mainly a positive impact on work climate. However, the suitable leadership style for a corporation may borrow segments of attributes of more than one of the above styles. In any case, practitioners must implement strategies and styles considering business ethics and their impact on individuals and other entities of the organization's internal and external environment.

Likewise, management styles can be indicated through individualism and collectivism. Individualism refers to the extent to which practitioners and their policies are focused on the rights and capabilities of individuals, whereas collectivism concerns the extent to which management policies are directed toward the development of employees, in terms of allowing them to participate in the management decision-making process (Purcell 1987). Management style, however, is different from management attitudes, as management is about behaving administratively and not creatively; thus, managers do not have the authorship to act on the basis of their personal beliefs and values necessarily.

It is worth mentioning that neither leadership nor management styles are equal to behaviors that can certainly be characterized as ethical or unethical. Therefore, both leadership and management can satisfy corporate and individual needs, depending on the selection and modification of the style that is most suitable for achieving organizational goals. What matters is how effective the selected style can be toward corporate people and the society in which they operate. Hence, moral leadership and management implies that individuals act considering the other entities involved or are affected by their behavior in the light of rapidly changing environments. There are a plethora of differences between leaders and managers based on their conceptualizations and approaches to work, underlying philosophies, and outcomes (Toor and Ofori 2008). A summary of the key differences between leadership and management styles and attributes is provided in Table 5.1.

The most important difference is that leaders draw their power from their personal traits and attributes, whereas managers draw their power from their position and authority. Leaders behave more with their soul and heart rather than with their mind, and this could be either great or morally dangerous. Leaders are usually good managers, but managers do not have leadership qualities. However, in many cases, leaders are unable to provide a corporation with the required elements of rules and operating procedures, and, thus, influencing people is not enough for a corporation to be sustainable and to avoid failure or even chaos. On the contrary, managers are guided mostly by handling routine in order to produce efficiency, and thus they are predictable, while leaders can create from the ground up inspiring policies and therefore produce value and generate new perspectives of corporate growth.

Businesspeople suggest that doing the right things is a leader's capability, whereas doing things right is about management. There are some attributes and skills that are not universally teachable, such as how to produce a vision or being effective by influencing instead of controlling other individuals. The same concept of internal driving forces in the context of business ethics leads to short-time or even instant behaviors without the need for additional moral analysis. This, however, can be achieved by both leaders and managers, because it is the individual entity that can be moral or unethical. It is crucial to understand that ethics cannot be applied if your internal world cannot be expressed by them. Obtaining the leader or manager label is not enough to be moral, and ethics must not be associated with the job role of an individual. On the other hand, ethics

Table 5.1   Leadership and management differences

Leaders	Managers
Are change agents, select talent, motivate, coach, and build trust.	Are principally administrators, plan, budget, evaluate, and facilitate.
Are strategists, original, visionary, passionate, creative, flexible, inspiring, innovative, courageous, imaginative, and experimental.	Are tacticians, rational, consulting, persistent, problem solving, tough-minded, analytical, structured, deliberate, authoritative, and stabilizing.
Ask what and why.	Ask how and when.
Are synonymous with becoming yourself.	Are becoming what company wants you to become.

and *moral entity consideration,* as a vital concept and point of reference, must be applied by anyone in a corporation and a society.

For instance, during a financial crisis, corporations suffer from scandals, including bribery, fraud, or corruption, and in some cases, these scandals lead to both financial and reputational losses if the corporation is involved in illegal or unethical activities. It has often been said that a financial crisis is an ethical crisis, so the latter is regularly presented as a crisis of leadership or management. A bribe is a gift of money or other inducement or a consideration offered with the explicit intention of causing an individual to violate his or her role obligations. It is likely that many of the inappropriate behaviors in the crisis are related to the existence of perverse incentives. Such unethical practices and policies push aside business ethics as greed and personal interests overcome fair judgment and *moral entity consideration.*

Legal behavior is not the same as ethical behavior. The activities that were employed before the implosion of the financial markets in 2008 were not against the law, but they were unethical, and they produced great harm and were contrary to ethical principles such as responsibility, transparency, and fairness (Trevino and Nelson 2014). Additionally, according to an inquiry report published by the U.S. government, "[W]e witnessed an erosion of standards of responsibility and ethics that exacerbated the financial crisis. This was not universal, but these breaches stretched from the ground level to the corporate suites. They resulted not only in significant financial consequences but also in damage to the trust of investors, businesses, and the public in the financial system" (FCIC 2011, 22). Corporate people bolstered the financial crisis, because borrowing money became cheap and this low cost of borrowing made it possible for everyone, without exception, to exploit this situation temporarily. For instance, the inquiry report mentioned that "the percentage of borrowers who defaulted on their mortgages within just a matter of months after taking a loan nearly doubled from the summer of 2006 to late 2007," showing that profit was the leading force for many individuals and corporations as entities, such as financial institutions.

This unethical situation and the implementation of unethical practices led to an unprecedented negative impact across the international economy. Leaders and managers tried to exploit the precrisis wealth, for their personal or corporate interests, whereas consumer savings dipped into negative territory. Responsible borrowers should have thought about what they could afford rather than what the banking system would lend to them, because of these policies. Also, lenders should have at least a second scenario that could make things sustainable again if borrowers could not afford to pay back the loans. Policy makers claimed that the unchecked increase in the complexity of mortgages and securitization has made it more difficult to solve problems in the mortgage market and hence it has reduced transparency for policy makers, regulators, financial institutions, and homeowners.

Therefore, sensitivity to business ethics must be adopted in times when a corporate is either in a crisis or in a well-established situation. If you gradually abandon and forget ethics when things are going well, then your modified moral principles are not enough to achieve a great and balanced business culture. As a manager, and particularly as a leader, you should have the capacity of moral thinking, being the entity of reference in a corporation. This state of self-regulation must be concerned with a strong ethical background, or else it could be critical and costly for both the legal entity and the individual. Consequently, supervisory authorities must be able to adequately identify the unethical behavior and promote ethics as a vital launching point to rectify any distortions in a corporation.

Moral leadership and management do not have the option of choosing whether a decision and corporate policy must be morally acceptable. For instance, the risk of contagion was an essential cause of the globalized crisis in 2008. The financial system was vulnerable and unable to react because "policymakers were afraid of a large firm's sudden and disorderly failure triggering balance sheet losses in its counterparties" (FCIC 2011, 419). These institutions, as many other private corporations around the world, were deemed too big and interconnected to other firms through counterparty credit risk for policy makers to be willing to allow them to fail suddenly. This shows that they implemented unethical practices to save both their corporations and the universal system in which they had strong relations and financial bonds. When a part of the chain fails, the latter breaks down completely with perhaps extremely negative consequences for the global financial system.

The banking system, monetary policies, and the complexity of the corporate competitive environment lead agents to behave unethically in many cases, in the name of securing a balanced and consistent environment for economics of a given society. The prevention of such crises is mostly inevitable due to the human nature of exploiting resources and circumstances to derive as much benefit as people can. However, this does not mean that practitioners have an unwritten rule to implement unethical policies that allow them to conveniently forget about the rationale and morality of their policies and practices. For instance, if the government policy had not been supportive of directing money into the mortgage markets in order to foster growth in homeownership, the 2008 financial crisis might have been prevented, because corporations would not have had such profit margins focusing on this market, and, consequently, this would not have triggered the creation of a bubble.

In any case, ethics must not be the reason for a failure or the main factor in generating conflicts. Instead, even though it is impossible to control everyone and develop a universal moral identity, it is feasible to eliminate such practices through rational corporate policies. Hence, moral leadership and management is about creating a comprehensive system of administration that enables the capabilities of the given resources, considering ethical principles and the rights of other entities.

Compensation Fairness and Ethics

At this point, it is worth noting one more critical issue, namely, wage management in the context of business ethics. Since the start of capital concentration, vesting the owner of the capital with the ultimate capability of distributing wages and allocating income, human resources have been the epicenter of the age-old question regarding whether an individual's income is fair and equal to his or her contribution to the organization. One of the most crucial questions emerging from this assumption is that of executive compensation.

Corporate executives, such as managers and leaders, get paid greater amounts of money annually, in comparison with lower level employees. In consequence, a smaller amount of capital may need to be distributed to the total headcount of human resources of the corporation, signifying that they get quite smaller portions of corporate profit. Executives may receive salary in terms of money, bonuses, grants of stocks, and other options such as retirement benefits and plans related to long-term productivity, and thus their package of benefits may be many times as much as the typical worker in the corporation is paid. Additionally, the compensation package of managers and leaders may increase considerably over time, whereas workers' pay remains stable or is increased by only a few points.

Indeed, it is expected that top managers are generally interested in increasing their pay; many top managers earn more on the first workday of the year than the average employee in their organization earns for the entire year, while pay dispersion between top managers and other employees is dependent, in part, on the ownership structure of their firms (Connelly, et al. 2016). This is critical considering that overpaying CEOs (chief executive officers) may have a negative financial performance impact (Fong 2010) on the firm, while pay ratio disclosure affects the purchase intentions of consumers via perceptions of wage fairness (Mohan, Norton, and Deshpande 2015). Additionally, most studies use the ratio of management to worker pay in an attempt to evaluate a firm's ethical pay, which could result in a variety of conflicts.

Is it possible, therefore, to determine whether a manager gets paid too much? Is it possible to evaluate the contribution of an executive? Or, in other words, is it fair to evaluate and judge what should be the income of a capital concentrator, considering that without him or her it would be more difficult for a single individual to create such employment conditions? For instance, the executive of a corporation is the one who will buy and sell goods and services by making the negotiations and agreements with suppliers, partners, and consumers, and he or she is confronted with additional responsibility in terms of being the legal representative of the organization. Also, executives are accountable for the creation of employment conditions, because they provide workers with job opportunities, while they must treat them as fairly as possible. The degree of responsibility increases the amount of pressure and risk on executives considerably, so some benefits must be given back to them. The latter are regularly translated into monetary terms, or other benefits associated with services or goods, and it is important to mention that there is a strong link between CEO pay and performance, especially when institutional owners have a large equity share (Bell and Reenen 2013). This is fair, although it must take into consideration a reasonable pay floor for well-being and good living.

Thus, when analyzing compensation fairness, a critical question emerges: How can an executive exclude the possibility for individuals to create such conditions, considering that if income distribution schemes were sustainable for them, they could have the capital required for micro entrepreneurship? The common characteristic of the above conditions is that of money-driven systems. This indicates that the leader or manager, as an executive individual with increased duties within a corporation, has an extended set of actions and responsibilities and thus must get paid more than the typical workforce. However, how much more consists of an ethical payment? How much more money does an individual need in order to live better than others and feel more comfortable and satisfied? How much luxury do they need? Do they deserve this amount of money?

Practically, no one deserves millions while others get only a few hundreds, or even nothing. This is not only unethical but also violative of the principles of fairness and meritocracy among equal members of a society. However, if we explore this assumption deeper, we soon realize that the contribution of some people is greater than that of other individuals. Thus, some people must get paid a higher amount of income, because ethics demands that equal payment must be given only to equal contributions of work. We need a hierarchical system of payment, because it gives a direct indicator of comparison in terms of contribution. But some people still get paid a lot more than they deserve. And it must be mentioned that payment inequalities are quite common not only at the executive level, but at all levels of employment, from the first-line worker up to the top manager and the owner of an organization. For instance, the holder of a company in retail industry may end up having a much smaller amount of income in comparison with the owner of another company in a similar situation and corporate revenue conditions, because of different circumstances and financial situations. Hence, who is responsible for the payment of an executive or the CEO? Who is responsible for deciding who deserves what level of payment?

Apparently, an authorized entity or a governmental instrument that is responsible for the level of payments does not exist. Governments are authorized to set only the minimum wage levels in a country, given that there must be a minimum level of payment for living. This payment is usually the first payment to an individual for an entry-level job role or an individual with the minimum background in terms of education and experience. Practitioners consider this minimum wage level in their policies, but there is no level at which the higher salary could be limited. Thus, the leader of a company, and generally the agents responsible for setting the wage structure of a corporation, have the authority to determine the wage levels of individuals. This structure relates to payments from the entry-level workers up to the executives. However, the payment of the owner or, in general, the shareholders in terms of merit is usually associated with the financial condition of a corporation and not necessarily with a contract with predefined and determined terms. Hence, it is noticed that when a company records a higher level of profit, so does the wage level of the owner, and, accordingly, when the company records a lower level of financial profit, or even losses, so does the income level of shareholders.

The ethical awareness of the pay structure mentioned emerges when the corporation records great levels of profit. Particularly, on the one hand shareholders keep this profit for their benefits, while on the other low-level workers do not see any increase to their income, or the increase is very small in comparison to shareholders' benefits. This is a constant issue and challenge in the business world ever since the establishment of the very first organization. The contract of an individual is associated with his or her educational background, experience, and other skills or attributes related to the individual's contribution to the organization. The benefit increase between the rather different levels of pay is related to specific productivity and efficiency rates, while there could be additional factors of pay increase at the same level of workers, such as in the case of those with families. The extra pay could be explained as a means of motivating workers or as an attempt to attract potential workers, because they need additional clauses to their contract in order to accept the position offered to them and get the job role.

However, as mentioned earlier, executive compensation is associated with the extensive range of responsibilities over corporate procedures, as well as with the high-risk level of their position and duties. This suggests that a position that stresses the individual a lot more than the usual and that puts pressure that could have negative consequences on the individual's life balance, the level of self-control, and the effort to retain a healthy mind operation is critical for the individual. Thus, it is morally acceptable to record pay levels of executives that are much higher than those of a typical worker, whereas the difference and ratio between the top and bottom pay levels in a corporation are determined through morally specific revenue and profit indicators.

While pay compensation benefit is vital for human resources, particularly when they are closer to the minimum level of wage, the debate on this challenge consumes valuable time on creating conflicting interests. Thus, it is essential to modify the level of compensation according to moral data and measures. Ethics suggests that when the contribution of an individual is similar—or mostly similar to—the contribution of another, the benefit package should be the same—or mostly the same—as well. This is why compensation fairness relies so much on the measurement instruments available to practitioners when they make plans on how to morally distribute the capital among human resources, although there is no universal guide to adhere to.

So can these corporate instruments consider and indicate the amount of contribution, in terms of responsibility or duties that present a high level of risk? Is it feasible to measure the impact of an idea to corporate efficiency? For instance, practitioners have the capability to measure the time an individual needs to do the same amount of work in comparison with the time needed by another individual. In this case, they can easily evaluate the contribution and take decisions about the pay level in relation to efficiency rates. Hence, when nonexplicit attributes are associated with pay level, and they need to be considered in the context of compensation fairness and ethics, corporate policies must be rational enough as well as capable of providing particular explanations as to why the compensation package of an individual is larger than that of another individual.

No one is authorized to take advantage of his or her position in order to have greater benefits that are against the benefit of others, but everyone deserves to record an increase in terms of pay levels analogous to the increase in the level of contribution. There are some leaders with a clear vision, innovative ideas, and pioneer contribution to a corporation, while there are also individuals who are satisfied with money-driven compensation, but they do not contribute to organizational goals. Some individuals need money to invest in infrastructure and human resources, whereas other people want money and concentrate capital merely on personal satisfaction and lifestyle. Although it is impossible to distribute production instruments into very small market share pieces, because this would make it irrational and insufficient to produce goods and services, it is feasible to create corporate policies, regulations, and law that could promote the process of fair pay among individuals.

Ethical Behavior Evaluation

The evaluation of ethical behavior as a very demanding and challenging process is directly related to agents, because they are responsible for conducting reviews, evaluations, and statements about performance and efficiency rates. Among numbers and statistics, there are also qualitative statements on behaviors, as an individual can have a strong impact on other entities and the work climate, thus decreasing the corporate value. Agents must prepare a list of agreed behaviors and evaluate what is done in practice, given a specific period. This process can be conducted annually, once a quarter, or monthly, depending on corporate needs and workflow procedures. Also, it is important to bear in mind that evaluation statements include data from daily operations and behaviors, and thus employees should always act ethically, and not only during the evaluation period. Hence, moral awareness is critical.

Practitioners must conclude a comprehensive statement and form approaches about the reasons for noting ethical or unethical behaviors. They must decide which unethical actions should be handled first, and what further steps must be undertaken to overcome such practices. Individuals must be given a fair explanation and be well informed of what they did that is characterized as unethical. Agents must avoid any misleading information, because it gives rise to objections. Additionally, it is important to mention that business decisions are made by individuals, and thus the ethics of business are the ethics of the individuals making up the business (Fritzsche 1991). So the indication must be clear, based on factual evidence, not opinion, and must be presented in a manner that enables individuals to recognize their unethical behaviors, accept their mistakes, and develop skills that put limits on these actions, following a flexible set of guidelines for behavior evaluation, as presented in Table 5.2.

Empowering the workforce is a mandatory process. Corporate agents must implement policies that provide good feedback to individuals and create a positive business culture that enables ethical behavior. Communication plays a critical role in this process, because dialogue between two or more interested and involved parties can result in a positive conclusion. Indeed, people need appreciation and trust; thus, practitioners must treat everyone with fairness and respect for merit, by providing rewards and warning recommendations where needed. The discussion must be open ended, and self-assessment must be promoted. It is also important to note behaviors immediately, because they can be the reason for a chain of reactions that cannot be stopped without vast losses if the situation goes far beyond corporate fundamentals.

Ethics relies on common norms and beliefs, although there are aspects that are largely subjective, and it is difficult to achieve consistency between rather different individuals. This implies that it is almost impossible to create a sustainable and fair business culture without balancing the different perceptions among individuals and considering a complex set of factors having a negative or influential impact on corporate performance. Monitoring people is not the same as evaluating machines. Some people may be strongly affected by criticism, and thus practitioners must be reasonably considerate with them, whereas other individuals need

Table 5.2   Ethical behavior evaluation model

Phases	Practitioner's reaction
Phase 1	At first, identify the unethical behavior. It is important to realize and analyze the problem, thus creating a feedback information package that helps all involved parties to understand.
Phase 2	Whether an individual is well motivated or well educated, an unethical behavior can occur, even by accident. Hence, the practitioner is responsible for exploring the conditions that have contributed to the unethical action.
Phase 3	In this final phase, the practitioner must decide and agree with all parties involved on what actions are required to create a new balance point, aligned with corporate policies. This process must be followed by monitoring the progress and creating new feedback channels.

some additional pressure to become efficient and well-motivated, because they need channels of challenges that empower them to create value and behave ethically.

Consequently, unethical behavior in business is not a recent phenomenon, while the most important factor in achieving ethical behavior in an organization is commitment by top management to that objective (Clement 2006). Therefore, practitioners must communicate behavior misalignments, monitor and evaluate actions that need to change, define simple and comprehensive expectations in the context of corporate policies, and ensure that everyone is informed and has the willingness to keep business culture positive and creative. This is a mandatory process, and practitioners must not underestimate the power of morals within business operations. The negligence of communication or consultation may lead to an unexpected decrease in corporate performance.

Concluding Remarks

Agency theory addresses the relationship between the principle and the agent and their conflicting interests. Investors employ agents to implement the corporate plan. Agents must be capable of making changes in their plans and policies, considering that people's perceptions cannot change instantly. Accordingly, the characteristics of leadership and management have a solid impact on employees' behavior and on overall business consistency. Leaders and managers must cope with microethical issues, while their control over ethical reasoning can be easily confused by external or internal factors. There is an extensive list of leadership and management differences, regarding their capabilities and authorities. Additionally, wage management and the development of a hierarchical system of payment is critical for the morality of a corporate structure, and an individual's income must be fair and equal to his or her contribution to the organization, including executive compensation. Finally, ethical behavior evaluation must be promoted as a process that secures ethics implementation and not as a demanding procedure that could only have a negative impact on work climate. Hence, individuals must build on a fair and rational set of corporate policies that enable their ethical behaviors.

PART III

Ethics and Employment Relations

This part is concerned with the moral factors affecting resourcing strategies, workforce planning, and people management. It examines the international characteristics of human resources, the instruments of moral employee management in fields such as motivation and commitment, and the important concept of ethical information management, in light of technological developments.

CHAPTER 6

Moral Workforce Planning

This chapter must begin with some critical questions: When was the last time you were evaluated by a third-party entity to get hired by an organization? What procedures did they implement, and what would you like changed for improved efficiency? Do you agree with the criteria that they followed as a recruitment guide for their corporation's needs? Do you believe that they were aligned with your internal moral principles and the corporate ethical code and that they were in accordance with corporate social responsibility? Did you have the opportunity to express your own beliefs, to be treated equally among rather different candidates, and judged in an ethical climate of communication and behavior?

All the foregoing recruiting issues and queries are crucial for conducting a moral workforce planning exercise, and a practitioner must consider multidimensional factors in the context of developing a moral thinking attitude. For instance, recruitment and selection, employee development, and employee reward policies need an advanced ethical plan on how to rationally exploit resources and improve corporate performance. Thus, a competency-based policy as an option related to business efficiency could deliver results while also being morally valid for both the corporation and society.

There are as many individual differences as there are individuals. Indeed, achieving a sustainable competitive advantage through corporate-specific competencies requires continuous monitoring because competency patterns may change over time (Lado and Wilson 1994). It is impossible and unsustainable to design organizational processes if individuals and other conditions are perceived as being basically the same; thus, people will behave rationally on any demand and corporate challenge, while other conditions remain unchanged. Internationalized training and education have limited the range of skill development, in terms of common educational programs and needs. However, globalization cannot universally erase culture and individual differences at a local level, so even with the very same education and training, or similar environmental information input, two individuals from the same local community will never present identical perceptions and therefore similar behavior.

People management would be tedious if individuals were the same. This is exactly why corporations cannot have a fixed and strict policy for any challenge posed. People cannot simply implement a procedure, particularly in the context of applying business ethics. Each operation is affected by the cultural perceptions in which people were brought up, their values and norms, gender, religion, emotions and feelings, abilities, and the variation of their skills, their intelligence level as well as their capacity for problem solving and abstract thinking, their conscientiousness, personal experiences, acceptance of change, self-awareness and self-management, their consistency over time, their expectations of the behavior of other people, and, finally, the external environment in which they behave, such as the economy, politics, and environmental conditions.

It is not discriminatory when you understand the existence of individual differences. Corporate unethical discrimination is about the unjust and prejudicial treatment of rather different individuals and categories of people. In particular, there are different types of discrimination, based on behavior. For instance, sexual harassment is about unwanted and repeated sexual advances and other physical or verbal conduct of a sexual nature, exclusion is about removing from certain individuals the opportunity to do specific tasks and jobs, intimidation is about bullying and threats between individuals or groups of people, incivility is about disrespectful treatment, including aggressive behavior, and, finally, mockery is about making jokes or expressing negative stereotypes that create conflicts between individuals. These unethical behaviors are fundamentally wrong and totally unacceptable, particularly if they consist of repeated actions of the same unethical behavior.

On the contrary, the ability to judge individuals by distinguishing their unique features is critical for providing fair and moral opportunities to everyone, because recognizing the differences of individuals in the context of business ethics leverages rational corporate efficiency. For instance, managing expatriates can be very challenging in terms of business ethics. Expatriates, that is, people working overseas, must be treated fairly as equal members of the corporation and the local society. Whether they agreed on short- or long-term contracts, expatriates must have the opportunity to contribute to the organizational operations by adopting new norms and working in unfamiliar but interesting environments.

The development of programs for expatriate individuals and making human resources available across borders is crucial, because this process enables corporations to increase their productivity levels and share practices. Corporations are exporting their core policies such as selection criteria, job role development, performance indicators, skills development, and training, by transferring knowledge to other individuals and corporations as entities worldwide through human resources. Additionally, it is important and beneficial for organizations to identify emotionally intelligent individuals to be sent on expatriate assignments, because high levels of emotional intelligence have a positive impact on cross-cultural expatriates, their performance, and general living (Koveshnikov, Wechtler, and Dejoux 2014). It is worth noting that some people feel like expatriates even in their home countries, because moving to another city within national borders is not very different from moving to another country entirely.

In any case, moving human resources to other locations for work is an inevitable process that many individuals must cope with. The management of expatriates can be a major factor determining business success or failure, because people must cope with new principles, colleagues, and business culture. It is necessary to treat expatriates and their families fairly, and this requires much more effort than language training alone. Indeed, relying on English as the dominant business language worldwide is inevitable, but this could be disadvantageous in terms of daily communication, which could lead to misunderstandings, particularly when the individual works for a nonmultinational company, where human resources may be required to use only English. Expatriates must challenge themselves with a new culture, including a wide range of information about local history, climate, politics, religion, society, and economics in the context of business, law, practices, and ethics.

It is also important to note that a multicultural approach is essential even for organizations operating locally. Different cultures can be found not only between employees of a multinational corporation, or the management of an organization with subsidiaries, but also among consumers. For instance, a local business in a city must serve the needs not only of local people but also of other individuals such as business partners abroad or tourists, with rather different cultural characteristics. This requires that individuals be well trained in order to behave ethically, equally, and in accordance with the code of conduct governing everyone.

Moral people management requires significant awareness of the motives of individuals. As already mentioned, individuals are different, presenting rather different attributes and personalities (Table 6.1). Motivation theories focus on expectations, goals, and equity of individuals. Maslow (1943) formulated a hierarchy of five needs, comprising physiological (lower level), safety-related, social, esteem-related, and self-actualization needs (higher level). He noted that if the basic physiological needs are unsatisfied, all other needs may become nonexistent or be pushed aside. Also, when a need is satisfied, another need emerges. However, it is possible to be partially satisfied from one need, and thus individuals do not wait until its fulfillment, as there are multiple determinants of behavior. For instance, financial incentives motivate many people, particularly in times of financial turmoil. Thus, given money as a powerful driving force, unethical policies, by providing money on unexpected terms, could be a useful but immoral stabilizing instrument. Money can change behaviors,

Table 6.1   *Individual variations*

Characteristic	Explanation
Intelligence and ability	Undeniably, individuals present different levels of education and knowledge, even if they have the same degrees and training inputs, due to variations in their intelligence capacities and personalities.
Expectations and planning	Individuals have their own path of development and have distinct expectations depending on personal plans and perceived experiences.
Values and norms	Values are beliefs about what is right or wrong to do, while norms provide informal rules on how to behave.
Environmental observance	People understand their environment differently and present different methods of adaptability.

motivate people with weak personality, and exploit humans in the best interests of the superior.

Conducting a moral workforce plan is a complex procedure for each organization. It demands a comprehensive strategy on team orientation to fit the right people to the right jobs and provide the proper training. The ability to be a fair member of an entity, with a full understanding of job roles and expectations on communicational behaviors, of the ability to manage and accept change when it emerges through variables such as financial or environmental issues, and of planning and organizing people management is vital for each corporation, so that people can develop trust, commitment, and interpersonal skills. Also, the capability of analyzing situations and evaluating alternatives is critical in a fast-paced business environment; hence, workforce plans must be aligned with logic, creativity, strategic schemes, and rational solutions.

Furthermore, it is very important to build an ethical employer brand, as was discussed in a previous chapter. This consists of a set of qualities and attributes that make a corporation appealing to candidates; creates a business culture of meritocracy, morality, and fairness; supports people as its core element of success; and increases its reputation to society. Organizations have their own core values, and they must be in accordance with generic norms in order to avoid being vulnerable to external criticism or judgment. The corporation must be a great place to work, not a place that someone needs to work due to money-oriented benefits. People need a work environment of excellence, opportunities for equal growth and promotions, an enhanced work–life balance, and a chance to be efficiently involved in corporate operations. Thus, business ethics is one of the most critical factors affecting employee retention and turnover. Indeed, considering ethical fitness, satisfaction and commitment are negatively related to turn over intentions, whereas satisfaction is positively related to affective commitment (Sims and Kroeck 1994). Additionally, other possible reasons for leaving could be the level of ethics implementation, work conditions and corporate climate, financial opportunities, better prospects, safety and security, poor relationships with colleagues and supervisors, the ability to cope with demanding tasks, harassment such as sexual harassment or racism incidents, or other personal reasons such as moving out of the area or pregnancy.

Depending on the corporate type of operations, needs, expectations, infrastructure framework, and other major factors such as its external environment, dealing with ethical workforce planning promotes commitment to the work, and encourages people to want to be part of the organization. Elimination of unpleasant work conditions is a mandatory process, while planning relies on flexible strategy. It is crucial to conduct plans according to different scenarios and prepare the corporation for any potential development. This rational process needs additional attention during workforce planning and research. For instance, it is impossible to recruit identical people, and thus their values and behaviors are different between rather different challenges. So a rational corporate policy could be to identify the core or cell of permanent employees who are essential to the ethical conduct of the corporation. This cell of perceptions must have the key skills needed to spread an efficient business culture to other individuals as well, by applying flexible and adaptable policies. Therefore, this cell of a corporation can enhance business ethics and productivity, and finally create a harmonious system of communication and cooperation between personal perceptions and business culture.

The establishment of a moral workforce planning is very important, as well as the examination of what we want, what we expect, and what kind of skills we need to achieve personal and corporate goals. Behavioral competences, such as moral skills, should be both role specific and related to an individual's perceptions, because it is crucial to ensure that candidates and, in general, the members of a corporation have the capabilities to fit, support, and enhance the organization's culture. A candidate's education and work experience are two of the most valuable elements of a biography; however, business ethics requires a lot more to be applied. If an individual with great attainments has a negative impact on others through his or her communication, behavior, or emotional conflicts, then corporate policies cannot ensure sustainability by themselves.

There are many more things to consider, such as an individual's intellectual capacity, moral awareness, social behavior (including online social behavior and reactions), communicational skills, availability, mobility, consistency on educational and employment history, acceptability of change and diversity, adaptability (including technology adoption), dependability, influence over other entities, commitment and engagement willingness, emotional stability, appearance, health (mental health related to family or other circumstances), motivation, and determination to develop and succeed. However, these features cannot be recognized equally by any individual, and thus it is important to have the right people in the right positions in order to ensure that they are aligned to corporate policies, so they will recruit candidates with shared perceptions.

It is impossible to attract candidates by placing advertisements mentioning that the corporation needs people with advanced morals. Which candidate will deny this? Furthermore, who will be responsible for identifying the moral level of an individual? Not only is this a demanding process, but technology and advanced machines with artificial intelligence and machine learning capabilities are working alongside practitioners to analyze a series of attributes and behaviors. Candidates want the job for their personal reasons. Practitioners must be capable of exploiting all available resources to locate the right candidates and treat them fairly and rationally.

Moreover, the individual interview is maybe the most familiar method of selection worldwide. It involves face-to-face communication and discussion of issues about job roles, opportunities, contract terms, and other specialized work conditions and policies. However, an interview alone cannot provide all the important information that a moral workforce plan requires. The predetermined questions cannot cope with real-time description of various topics during a discussion between two or more individuals. Thus, the interviewer must have a strong internal driving force in terms of ethics and an enhanced set of communicational skills to conduct and analyze unstructured interviews. Also, the disadvantage of biased and subjective judgment by the interviewer can lead to undesired actions. Therefore, the discussion must be taken in the context of ethical consideration, from evaluating a candidate to informing him or her of the result, whether positive or negative.

It is important to note that there are intelligence tests as well, but they are mostly useful to identify skills, critical thinking capability, and knowledge capacity, rather than ensuring the moral identity of a candidate. The latter, if he or she is well prepared, can hide unethical behavior and thoughts, and thus open-ended written or oral questions are required to unveil such practices. Preparation is essential, and this indicates that behavioral questions are critical as well. For instance, you can ask the candidate directly whether trust and commitment are important for him or her and how he or she reacts under tremendous business pressure to achieve a result, in the context of being efficient and ethical at the same time. Tests must meet criteria for reliability and validity, because they are helpful when intelligence is a key factor, although they have limits in terms of providing behavioral attributes, as mentioned.

Moral Resourcing Design

Establishing a strong and enhanced business ethics code begins with the development of a moral resourcing design. When a practitioner analyzes corporate jobs, roles, and competencies needed to achieve organizational goals, moral awareness must be a key factor. Designing a job is critical for corporate success and harmony. In particular, not only is designing a moral job crucial, but it fundamentally consists of a multidimensional process of defining a set of tasks and activities that are ethically suitable for both the individual that will accept to do the job and the corporation that designs and offers it. Job description must be aligned with corporate ethical principles, whereas the job role analysis must contain flexible terms reflecting the ever-changing demands and morals.

Undeniably, corporations need different kinds of competencies and human skills for different jobs. However, organizations must not implement policies that are against individuals that cannot follow business change instantly, or that have their unique set of morals or expectations. It is not ethical and fair to modify job roles without communicating the changes to the individuals that they involve or demanding different skills from rather different employees for the same job description and role. It is reasonable to consider personal specifications for setting a different set of rules, but this policy must give everyone equal opportunities without exceptions.

For instance, during an interview it is unethical to treat a potential employee with additional pressure and undue stress, while treating another candidate with flexibility, in order to recruit the individual that you want. Business ethics relies on equality and integrity, not on preferences based on personal perceptions and behaviors of ruling or even manipulating other entities. The job analysis interview must be conducted in the context of moral awareness, promoting logic over control. When you conduct an interview, you must think of the behaviors and questions that you would want to see from your interviewer. Thus, this simple principle helps to identify whether a behavior may be acceptable, at least from one's point of view, depending on the level of ethical awareness of practitioners.

Interview questions can have a positive or negative impact during the process of selection. Although there are no interview questions that are illegal from an ethical standpoint, there are questions that can make an individual feel disadvantaged and, consequently, make the conversation nonprofessional. This implies that some questions may lead to moral discrimination. Before citing a few examples of questions that are discriminatory, it is important to argue that certain questions may be unacceptable for some individuals, but good to know for others, and in their best interests. For instance, why should the question seeking to know the number of children, if any, be considered unacceptable? If the corporate policies promote benefits for individuals with children, then this must be not only an acceptable question but also an ethical one, because if the practitioner does not ask the individual about his or her personal status, then it could be discriminatory in relation to other individuals who may voluntarily mention that they have children, in order to receive any potential benefits, although the right not to unveil your personal status is always acceptable and morally understandable.

Therefore, questions regarding job role demands and compensation benefits must be addressed in terms of implementing a fair interview policy. Additionally, for most, if not all job positions, it is important to employ people with a minimum educational background needed for a task. This suggests that you have the right to ask for someone's degree and other qualifications. But is it unethical to ask when he or she graduated from high school or university? For instance, if candidates graduated very many years ago and if since then their experience and positions in which they worked were unrelated to their degree, it could mean that they may now not have the skills they had in the past. This is critical in terms of efficiency, whereas the question of whether someone can perform the duties of the job that he or she applied for could not end with the appropriate answer. Thereby, some individuals reply positively even if they lack the educational or experience background needed. This would mean that some people, in order to be hired and get the job, are lying in an unethical attempt to convince the interviewer. Thus, in the name of business ethics, it is not rational to avoid such questions and make unethical decisions against other individuals and the corporation itself as an entity.

Accordingly, it is important to ask questions about his or her availability and what days and hours they can work, whether there are any specific demands for personal reasons, and whether they are legally eligible for employment in the country that the corporation operates in. In light of this, for some people it is unacceptable to be asked for their citizenship and national origin as a criterion for selection, but this is inevitable because it will be revealed in terms of a contract and other bureaucratic requirements such as tax-related statements and procedures according to national law. Using racially balanced interview panels is critical in order to give an appearance of fairness to all candidates (Prewett-Livingston, et al. 1996), because racial labor market disparities persist across nearly all stages of the employment process (Pedulla and Pager 2019). Also, during an interview it is unethical to ask about their parents' citizenship or question their financial status in terms of whether they have real estate or other property or ask about their past wages. This is not a job requirement, so it is unethical and unacceptable, while the candidate always has the right not to answer. You cannot ask an individual about which societies or other communities he or she belongs to, but it is very important to ask about membership of an association related to skills that are relevant to his or her ability to perform the job.

Every individual is different, having distinct expectations, and reacts uniquely. Practitioners must increase their capacity to think flexibly, because it is their responsibility to form a communicational style of mutual respect and morality. During recruitment, you must treat candidates with ethical consideration, and keep them informed without undue delay of decisions made about their application, give them feedback about results, unless there are explicit reasons not to do so, provide a reasonable chance and time to ask whatever they want about the job and work climate, and not keep them waiting for the interview. Also, give them accurate and complete information about job requirements and roles and about the terms and conditions of employment. Moral resourcing relies on the practitioner's ability not to criticize aspects of a candidate's character and personal experiences, or at least not to express them harmfully to the individuals. Undeniably, when someone meets another individual and starts discussing a variety of topics, sooner or later a comprehensive opinion can be evolved.

At this point, there is a critical question, namely, whether you must cooperate with an individual with whom you have no common reference points. Is it ethically acceptable to believe that two individuals will cooperate smoothly, just because they are required to do so by corporate performance standards? No, this is not a moral resourcing design. Sometimes, you must sacrifice a small part of financial return in order to enhance corporate culture and human well-being, with respect for individual rights, beliefs, self-esteem, communication style, privacy, and autonomy. In any case, organizational policies must not manipulate people into accepting imposed corporate values and principles.

An ethical resourcing design like the one presented in Table 6.2 can be very helpful for implementing rational corporate policies. The description of the main and side activities and duties must be aligned with solid ethical principles, in terms of providing as much information as possible about how to behave and retain a moral act, without harming other entities. Collaboration between individuals must be efficient, and they must agree on the purpose of their activities, priorities, and expectations concerning their outputs or moral standards that they should achieve.

Table 6.2   Ethical resourcing design

Term	Ethical dimension
Job title	The job title must be understandable by both parties, rational, and acceptable since the beginning.
Authority	A candidate who is being hired must know to whom he or she is responsible and who is responsible to him or her.
Expectations and activities	This part of resourcing design must be clear and rational. It sets the overall terms that both the individual and the corporation are expected to meet. It is at least unacceptable to change expectations or activities first agreed to unless both parties agree on new arrangements.
Rewards	Benefits must reflect performance, skills, and predefined conditions. They must not be changed unless both parties agree on new arrangements.

The aim of a corporation must be to ensure that it achieves competitive advantage by attracting, retaining, and developing more capable human resources than its rivals. Employing and organizing people effectively is a mandatory process for corporate success. Thus, the workforce must have a wider and deeper range of both skills and internal moral principles in ways that can maximize its contribution to organizational goals. This indicates that corporate decision makers must have the skills needed to resource people whose behaviors and attitudes are within the context of what agents believe to be suitable for the corporation.

If we take this one step further, agents must not hire people that are aligned with their personal perceptions, as this increases the possibility of staffing the corporation with people that cannot cooperate. This demonstrates that you cannot have two leaders for the same task, you cannot employ two technical experts and let them try to compete with each other in unethical practices, and you cannot create a dysfunctional culture with dissatisfied individuals. Therefore, skills hunting is useful just as the first-level approach. You then need to design a rational and moral policy, which involves finding both skills and behaviors that can serve business needs efficiently and negotiating employment terms in good faith.

Workforce and Technological Age

Taking advantage of the smart features of technology, notably artificial intelligence and machine learning, recruitment and evaluation processes can be carried out by automated systems. This implies that the corporation has the capability, in the context of the fourth industrial revolution, to authorize technology to act voluntarily, without human intervention, beyond supporting recruiters in making the final decisions (Mantzaris and Myloni 2018). However, will a machine ever be able to measure in computerized data on human creativity, motivation, passion, moral principles, problem-solving capabilities on human issues, judgment, critical thinking, human sense, trust, personality, and emotions? Although artificial intelligence and machine learning techniques are quite capable of doing immersive analysis based on inputted data, human moral thinking cannot be analyzed in algorithms, because it is such a complex and multidimensional process that no human can be conceptualized into machine intelligence.

During workforce planning, we do not need to consider whether the comparative advantages of a robot are more than human or whether the reverse is true, as major moral issues emerge. Instead, we need to focus on optimal efficiency through the resources that the corporation needs, thus developing a plan that enhances both factors equally and ethically. As far as corporate performance is concerned, both humans and machines can add value to an organization, so the combination of both is the key to business sustainability and development in the age of technological explosion. Specifically, moral resourcing is about attracting and retaining high-quality people by giving everyone equal opportunities of employment. However, resourcing in the technological age is about attracting and retaining high-quality, future-oriented, and skilled candidates, in the context of innovative skills, fast-paced learning capabilities, motivation for constant change and self-development, and willingness to contribute to the machine–human relationship.

Attracting candidates is a process that requires flexible and multidimensional corporate policies. As mentioned previously, technology plays a significant role, so practitioners must rationally exploit the available innovative applications. You should not be attracted by candidates that sell themselves by mentioning utopian achievements. Thus, in cases where difficulties in evaluating candidates are being encountered, practitioners must employ technology and expose the real characteristics and achievements of candidates and identify any hidden weaknesses that need improvement. For instance, it is fair to ascertain the validity of their qualifications or expose candidates to short knowledge tests, aptitude tests, intelligence tests, or personality tests. A knowledge test can prove an individual's current training and capabilities, an aptitude test can explore the extent to which the candidate can do the job, an intelligence test can measure a range of critical mental abilities that enable the candidate to succeed at a variety of demanding corporate tasks, and there are also personality tests that attempt to assess the personality of candidates in an effort to predict and understand their intentions and likely behavior as part of the organization. Additionally, living in the digital age allows one to search for further information on their social network profiles or the candidate's own blog and other electronic sources. Remember that you must search only for job-related attributes such as achievements, biographical data, publications, or skills and that you must not violate personal information and digital data that are in the context of private life under the auspices of general data protection regulation (GDPR).

It is crucial to consider whether you violate their privacy and personal data. Corporate policies must stop at the point where they violate individual privacy by demanding personal details that are not related or required within the context of employment relationship. Therefore, it is important to develop policies that build trust upon privacy and not make individuals feel uncomfortable about their personal data. In view of this, it is inevitable to avoid data exposure, because in the technological age almost everyone accepts terms and conditions online or offline without even reading them. But, at least in a corporate environment, practitioners must treat their workforce better than a mere means of the system.

Technological advancements such as artificial intelligence can be exploited by avoiding part of the foregoing tests, because smart technology can search online material and summarize the electronic presence of the candidate. However, technology must be well programmed, structured, reliable, valid, and accurate, based on specific criteria, particularly considering data privacy. Therefore, the process for the final selection of the right person for the right job could be done manually, machines being known to be, in some cases, subject to human bias, while reliance on machine automation and automated decision aids can result in automation bias (Wall, et al. 2018), and thus individuals could deceive technology to serve their own interests. For instance, technology cannot completely understand human emotional communication yet, while it is important to consider that there are many promising ways of implementing visualization of a subject's emotional state in real time through advanced machine learning techniques (Wang, Nie, and Lu 2014). Hence, evaluating applications and candidates with a human sense is a characteristic that could be beneficial even in the age of artificial intelligence, but this must be done through a valuable interconnection with intelligent applications.

Furthermore, because of the amount of information available online and in order to save time and cost, corporate policies could be secured with some alternatives. Practitioners can provide clear statements on what they ask in the initial application and also agree with the candidate that was the best fit for the job to sign terms on potential facts and behaviors that could disrupt and distort corporate culture. This is a rational and ethical policy that facilitates resourcing strategy, while it defends corporate core values and principles. However, as it is impossible to predict any potential future challenges, this process must have flexible characteristics as well, regarding ethical awareness, emerging issues, and mutual interests.

Equal and Ethical Opportunities

Career management, talent management, and people management are categorized into different definitions for the same core factor: the human. This signifies that people are at the epicenter of business operations, and thus their fair and moral treatment is the only way of developing a sustainable business culture and achieving organizational goals efficiently. Shaping the progression of individuals within an organization through rational and moral policies is crucial in order to balance the interests and preferences of both the individuals as members and the corporation as an entity.

Opportunities and guidance must be distributed equally among all corporate members and individuals' perceptions, expectations, and interests considered in conjunction with corporate needs and goals. This process and policy lead to the development of *moral entity consideration* throughout the career life cycle of individuals. Opportunities are not just for beginners. Indeed, the entry into an organization is usually the most difficult period of an individual, as he or she must adopt new conditions and become familiar with new roles and tasks. However, opportunities must be equally and morally given to people who are at a midcareer stage, or even at the end of their career.

Midcareer people need opportunities to take further steps and be well motivated, recognized, and rewarded for the progression of their career. If people lose interest at this stage, then it is very tough to return to the previous level of interest, because it requires additional effort to recover. Opportunities such as job rotation, special agreements, or even a move to another corporate segment may be the only way to achieve individual development, at this level of workforce planning. Furthermore, toward the end of the career of an individual, the possibility of being treated with unethical and unequal practices is significant. Many corporations, whether it is an unofficial policy, believe that it is better to convert contracts from full-time to part-time agreements, because they impart flexibility in terms of providing both work opportunities to aged people and room for leveraging younger employees. However, this process may lead to disengagement and decreased commitment levels, while splitting benefits may create additional issues, such as the level of pay. Treating people with respect, given that they are still making a fair contribution to corporate operations, is essential for building a moral culture. Moreover, their experience may be quite important for keeping a well-optimized business, because they can eliminate risks and enhance practices that have proved to be efficient in the past, although this must not eliminate the need for fresh ideas and new approaches.

Career decline is inevitable without the existence of a strong set of rational policies on people management. Growth cannot be enforced. It must be followed by individual willingness for change, expansion, and positive maturation. At the same time, corporate policies must include promotion statements related to specific achievements, thus letting individuals have the opportunity to move from the bottom to the top level of the organizational hierarchy. This can be achieved through the development of advanced skills and knowledge and the establishment of a comprehensive corporate system that rewards those individuals who contribute the most, by implementing fair policies in the context of meritocracy.

Furthermore, it is difficult to forecast the future needs of a corporation in terms of skills, and complicated to forecast the future of the employees in terms of their capabilities as well. Hence, practitioners must develop strategies and policies that plan career paths that the corporation will need in the future, thus securing business sustainability into an ever-changing environment. Here, it is essential to incorporate employee voice strategies to achieve better efficiency, as individuals may have the capabilities needed to exploit any opportunities that are offered. Employees can perform a greater part in the decision-making process by being given the opportunity to enhance policies, discuss the issues that affect them through employee involvement, and contribute to the improvement of the corporation.

This strategy emphasizes mutual gains as both parties are satisfied about the creation of a fair work climate of development, sustainability, and growth. The opportunity to make suggestions and be consulted during decision making is a process that enables employee commitment and leads to an increase in corporate efficiency, as this reinforces employees' sense of fairness and engenders greater trust in the organization (Rees, Alfes, and Gatenby 2013). Also, the right to veto a corporate decision is important, as well as the right to be well informed about agreements and policy terms. It is unethical to implement practices such as hiring people that you will manipulate for your own interests, without giving them an opportunity to develop their skills and positions. Neither is it ethical to want to be hired only to be part of a corporation with all its benefits and then create conflicts because you never actually wanted to work in such a corporate climate.

Hence, employee contribution must be secured, in an attempt to seek initiatives and handle potential conflicts at work. This process can be time consuming, so it is advisable to approach this by giving individuals enough time to respond to corporate proposals and receive meaningful material to consider. Time pressure can be a disastrous factor. Some individuals cannot deal with time management, deadlines, and processes that may affect other entities because they feel stressed under the pressure of heavy responsibilities. Undeniably, some individuals have a greater impact on corporate decisions than others, yet everyone must have an equal chance to express their willingness to act, such as an initiative.

People respond to conditions differently, owing to a variety of personality traits. For instance, talented individuals have the ability to develop themselves, are motivated, and are naturally curious. Some individuals possess strong emotional intelligence skills, enjoy new challenges and engagements, are confident, determined, have developed communicational skills, can manage stressful and demanding work environments, have advanced learning capabilities, and present creative problem-solving attributes, by adapting to new environmental trends and demands.

In contrast, other individuals need mentors because they want a supervisor to tell them what and how to do something, have less willingness to develop because they are not confident enough to overcome difficult situations, and could end up being a constant negative factor, by generating conflicts with others, in an attempt to feel recognizable and valuable. They are usually averse to change and are afraid of learning new things, because this process arouses feelings of fear and failure, forcing them to avoid such developments, or could end up behaving unethically in order to gain the attention of other individuals, even if this works to their detriment. Consequently, the corporate environment is influenced, shaped, and affected by some individuals, whereas others are followers. This is not a negative issue, because human differences demonstrate the development of such behavioral oscillations.

Concluding Remarks

People management would be tedious if individuals were the same. There are as many individual differences as there are individuals. Therefore, conducting a moral workforce plan is a complex procedure for each organization. A rational corporate policy could be to identify the core or cell of permanent employees who are essential to the ethical conduct of the corporation. In any case, when a practitioner analyzes corporate jobs, roles, and competencies needed to achieve organizational goals, moral awareness must be a key factor. Business ethics relies on equality, integrity, and promotion of logic over control. Practitioners must increase their capacity for flexible thinking but must not allow a dysfunctional culture to be created by unsatisfied individuals. Technological advancements could be used to achieve the best of workforce planning but must be part of a comprehensive decision-making procedure, including human sense. For instance, opportunities and guidance must be distributed equally among all corporate members, as a process that leads to the development of *moral entity consideration* all through the career cycle of individuals. Furthermore, employee contribution must be secured in the attempt to seek initiatives and handle potential conflicts at work.

CHAPTER 7

Ethical Information Systems

The computing power available for processing data from all around the globe has risen to a level at which fundamentally new corporate policies and practices of data analysis are emerging. For instance, monitoring the performance of individual work effort represents a significant cost for an organization, and inefficiencies are created when the flow of information on individual performance decreases (Alchian and Demsetz 1972). Thus, using advanced techniques such as machine learning and artificial intelligence that enable data scientists and professionals to harvest the available information in innovative ways is a mandatory corporate process. There is a crucial need for each business to develop systems and digital frameworks on which reliable information can be collected and analyzed such as employee productivity, flexibility in technology adoption, added value per measured unit, and behavior reflections on the factors of business culture and financial returns.

Developments in technology enable corporations to manage a huge amount of information. Indeed, organizations with services and applications such as search engine platforms, e-mails, personal messages apps, picture store depositors, and other cloud-based data know a lot more about us than we might have ever realized. Technological advances enable the management of information with multidimensional approaches. For instance, researchers demonstrate machine learning with advanced techniques that successfully identify people's emotional situation based entirely on real-time recordings of their facial expressions, voice tone, and speech (Wang, Nie, and Lu 2014). Thus, not only is this information extremely sensitive, but the amount of this information collected through computer vision and analyzed by artificial intelligence suggests that an individual is not isolated in terms of privacy and personal data. The age of distrust demonstrates that we will not be able to recognize whether a behavior is morally acceptable, when a human or a robot tells the truth, and whom to trust while trying to cope with demanding corporate dilemmas. Uploading your personal data to an interconnected technological system capable of analyzing anything through data science, whether done intentionally or not, must be brought under the lens of ethics and human intervention.

Although information overload is not just a matter of Internet and e-mails, in the presence of attention manipulation, competitive information supply can reduce consumer knowledge by causing information overload (Persson 2018). Considering this, information overload leads to the exploitation of technological applications—whether it be a personal notebook or a personal pocket-size computer, such as a smartphone—in an effort to always remain competitive and achieve corporate goals. However, using a personal device for corporate reasons can raise moral issues. In many cases, an individual uses his or her own mobile device for accessing private organizational information and applications. Thus, the corporation must develop an extended set of guidelines for cases where a personal device is lost or stolen to ensure that both individuals' privacy and corporate information will not be used against them by third-party entities. Furthermore, if an advanced machine is capable of thinking, who will be responsible for data management and control of machine behavior? Hence, emerging technologies can lead to many security and connectivity issues.

In addition, the variety of interfaces and experiences is increasing over time, and although we take advantage of technology, we are getting addicted to these elements of daily data control and management. The workforce is becoming more flexible, mobile, interconnected, and influenced by technology while increasing efficiency and adopting intelligent machines in its daily protocols and encounters. Corporate environments of previous centuries had no individual-level applications at all. During the early phase of industrialization of tools essential to produce outputs, such as a hammer, more efficiently, data management was never a problem. The human being was the only privileged entity capable of thinking, behaving, and evaluating policies and operations. However, the technological advancements of the last two centuries have changed almost everything in corporate policy making, and since then being ethical has not been a concern exclusive to human mandate any more.

Indeed, anything that can be digitized will be digitized, and thus it is crucial for practitioners to understand the implications of digitization for their organization and employees, considering that digitization accelerates the speed of change that companies are facing (Kohnke 2017). Algorithms support humans in deciding whom to hire, whom to promote, and what data to consider in order to act rationally in terms of profit maximization. However, artificial intelligence and advanced machines are not developed to produce values, opinions, and beliefs in a way that a human does. This is not the aim of artificial intelligence. If the creator of a system contributes to its core elements with personal prejudices, then human bias consists of a critical moral issue for technological implementation. Skewed data and technical limitations may slow down human displacement in many business sectors; however, the owners or holders of information and technology as a combination of tools that can lead to corporate excellence have a robust advantage against their competitors in the technological age.

The availability and storage of vast amounts of digital data is leading to the exploitation of the innovative capabilities of computing power. Artificial intelligence, machine learning, and other similar advanced technologies can quickly capture and analyze a wealth of physical and digital data that a human cannot even approach as an intelligent worker. Thus, a human worker would have to devote a lot more time to these complicated and demanding tasks in order to compete with machines. Under this pressure, technology is converting the worker into a 24/7 available employee for the employer through technological applications such as a simple e-mail, which connects two or more individuals instantly without geographical boundaries.

Furthermore, ethical concerns arise with the implantation of microchip technology inside the human body using electromagnetic fields to identify electronically stored data. This information system implants microchips that embody electronic control systems under the human skin or even in the brain in order to have wireless communication with computers. In particular, short-range wireless connectivity technology can use the capability of the human body to transport signals that provide intuitive, simple, and safe communication between two electronically compatible devices (Pop 2011). Health organizations have identified radio frequency electromagnetic fields as possibly carcinogenic to humans (Baan, et al. 2011); however, in some cases this could be a mandatory part of the employee's contract. This constitutes an extreme and critical ethical issue, because microchip implants can be used to provide the owner of technology with a tremendous amount of private data, and thus moral awareness must be ensured in many diverse fields.

Ethical Measurements

Information systems give practitioners and corporations the ability to concentrate an excessive amount of data about individuals. Starting with basic workforce data, according to record-keeping standards of most civilized countries across the world, employers gather various kinds of information such as demographic data, including the employee's full name, as used for social security purposes; the employee's identifying symbol or number if one is used in place of name on any time, work, or payroll records; address with zip code, birth date (depending on local law requirements), sex and/or gender (the difference has been analyzed in a previous chapter), time and day of week when the employee's workweek begins and ends, as well as contract arrangements such as total wages paid in each pay period and the date of payment. Practitioners can record the number of hours worked each day and workweek by individuals, the basis on which employee's wages are paid, and other additional information such as total overtime earnings.

Also, practitioners can gather through mandatory corporate procedures important information about the employee's skills and qualifications, work experiences, as well as perceptual data such as their social media posts concerning the work, and performance data on their financial and operational efficiency. Job roles and contract arrangements as data can be used for policy making on serving interests, and information about individuals' skills and performance can be used as a point of reference in exploiting the available resources efficiently to achieve organizational goals. Because this set of stored data can generate countless insights about individuals, ethical concerns arise, and corporate policy makers should focus on how to cope with the very vital issues of privacy and securitization of data. A summary of the most important measured data and their potential ethical uses is provided in Table 7.1.

The manageability of sensitive data is very important in establishing an ethical business environment. There is a broad array of metrics to gather, whose use may have a positive or negative impact on both the corporation and the individuals. The analysis of data must be done through a process of moral good and used in the context of building ethical business policies reporting on organizational aims and performance. Data must not be used for personal advantage or for the benefit of third parties. Evaluation of data must be accurate, trustworthy, valuable, integral, credible, and accompanied by advanced ethical principles driven by internal morals, corporate standards, and societal demands. You must imagine yourself in the position of the individual when you analyze his or her data and treat employee data as you would treat your personal sensitive information.

Therefore, in terms of security and privacy, corporations must uphold the best methods and practices, while refreshing their terms and conditions regularly. The system must be multilayered and include innovative applications such as encryption or enhanced blockchain technology. Policy makers must explain how they collect, use, exploit, analyze, and

Table 7.1   Possible moral use of data

Measured data	Possible use
Sex, gender, age, race, health, contract arrangements, education, skills, qualifications	Analyze diversity by various demographic factors; compose business culture policies, particularly for multicultural business environments; and build strategies on contract arrangements, skills, and corporate needs.
Employee efficiency rates and rewards	Indicate areas of success and failure, plan next steps that must be taken to increase efficiency. Control over reward policies and demonstrate a fair, equal, moral, and well-optimized system related to contribution.
Employee development and well-being	Indicate everyone's needs; make moral use of supervision, influence; lead, hear, respond, and formally behave. Assess and evaluate health and safety programs, and do not put performance over health.

share individuals' data. Also, corporate policies must allow individuals to control the use of their data through transparent procedures and always seek permission for sharing information with third parties. Furthermore, corporate policies must include a comprehensive set of guidelines on how to minimize biases and inaccuracies, which may have unintended consequences for individuals and society. Thus, they must be aligned with social values and be responsible for potential data corruption.

For instance, any decision to modify personal data must be based on the individual's consent, which should be provided in written form on paper or on electronic platforms. The employer must always be prepared to demonstrate, on request, that he or she has informed the employee, in accordance with law and ethics, and that the employee has the right of free choice, such as being able to refuse or withdraw consent, with no adverse consequences for him or her. Consent must be considered as a result of free choice, particularly where it is linked to a financial benefit to the employee or to the satisfaction of the employee under contract and labor law, collective bargaining and social security law, and the business ethics framework.

Another important example is the processing of personal data through a closed-circuit optical recording system within the workplace. This practice must be prohibited, considering that it violates human privacy and morals. Exceptionally, it could be permitted if necessary for the purpose of protecting persons and goods, and under specific circumstances by securing legal compliance. However, this implies that even if it is in the best interests of everyone at one place, individuals must be well informed and details must be provided as to what data has been gathered from authorities and corporate systems, for what reason, and how it will be exploited. In most cases, the law forbids data collected through a closed-loop optical recording system from being used as the sole criterion by which employee behavior and efficiency are evaluated.

Maximizing organizational performance through information management is essential for corporate success, as the effective analysis adds value to the decision- and policy-making process. The concept of performance measurement covers both what has been achieved and how it has been reached through resource exploitation. Data examination highlights possible barriers within business operations and individuals, while underlining utilization rates of resources and the strengths and weaknesses of each category of analyzed data. This process can be done with the support of key performance indicators (KPIs), which are regularly used to measure financial results and productivity. However, many corporations follow unethical policies aimed at bolstering efficiency, leading to the creation of poor working conditions and unrealistic corporate expectations. For instance, workers may be pushed to run and walk many hours or deal with injuries and unbearable fatigue, while having the time and speed of their movements and breaks measured for optimal efficiency. Also, some organizations unofficially equip workplaces with vending machines that provide stressed or injured workers with painkillers to meet their performance targets. These practices are both unethical and unpleasant for people, because they create an environment where human resources are exploited as mere tools, rather than being treated as valued entities with needs and demands.

E-Metrics and 360-Degree Ethics

Although technology presents great opportunities to advance, a key question arises: Why do we need to give so much attention to technological development and its relationship to business ethics? The answer is not simple. Technology enables the use of an extensive 360-degree feedback mechanism for all corporate procedures. This indicates that the human worker is not the only factor that can create value in business and society in general. Thus, 360-degree ethics relies on a multidimensional set of actions on how to retain ethics in a fast-paced globalized environment.

The 360-degree scheme is a relatively new and powerful feature of data management. Human resource information systems (HRIS) software presents the human resource function with new challenges (Dery, Grant, and Wiblen 2009). Advanced information systems have the capabilities to gather, analyze, and generate an enormous amount of data regarding anything that can be measured with quantitative and qualitative methods. They give practitioners a more rounded view of whatever they need to explore and evaluate. Thereby, they enhance the validity and acceptability of results, because the latter are rationally explained through data. The existence of such capable tools signifies that behaviors can be captured in the form of digital data as well. Consequently, the concentration of data constitutes an extremely effective tool for each corporation.

For instance, you can manage people with powerful software that gathers data such as the employee's photo, last name, first name, job title, location, employment status, personal webpage and social media links, e-mail, and phone number. You can group the directory by filters such as name, department, location, or division, and you can always do a search to find, export, and analyze employee data. Also, it is very helpful and useful to review the employee list through organizational charts. Consequently, individuals, as employees, have their own profile page inside a human resources software. As a result, you can find a wealth of data about your employees, including personal information, such as name, preferred name, birth date and age, ethnicity, social security number and tax-related information, sex, gender, marital status, address, contact data, education, experience, and even their clothing size, for marketing and formal dress purposes. In addition, information is available about their direct reports and the name of the manager whom each employee is associated with.

Moreover, software provides solutions to gather data about hire date, employee comments over the employment status, job information, compensation and other benefits, frequency and history, time-off timeline and scheduling, notes in the context of what colleagues and supervisors say about his or her behavior or performance, upcoming training, and onboarding and offboarding tasks. Also, most software applications have cloud service options, in terms of storing résumés and applications, signed documents, personal documents, task lists, and workflow attachments. Individuals are also associated with corporate assets, such as a computer, a smartphone, a tablet, or a desk phone. Thus, electronic metrics (e-metrics) provide data such as asset description, serial numbers of devices, and date loaned or returned. Hiring tools are also available, allowing you to organize job openings, candidate ratings, hiring status such as candidates reviewed, offers made, interviews scheduled, or put on hold.

It should also be noted that because of technological innovation and flexible work environment, many corporations equip workers with mobile phones, tablets, or laptops, enabling them to connect to the internet for business purposes when they are not in the office. However, sometimes they ask them to install a range of software that track user's movements.

Such software can records users' keyboard strokes and mouse movements, as well as the applications that they have open on their device screen. Some companies may ask for their workforce to even allow to install applications that take videos of users' screen or even user's face through the device camera to check if they are working.

In terms of biometric technologies and their ethical implications, an individual can be used as a unique identifier. This signifies that a human being can be characterized by a tag of recognition into the digital world of information. Biometric technologies refer to sensors and advanced systems used to identify individuals through a biometric. Biometric technologies use human-possessed biological (anatomical, physiological, and behavioral) properties to determine or verify an individual's identity (Wang and Yanushkevich 2007). This feature can be extremely useful to corporations. Since the first industrial revolution, biometric technologies have been one of the most prominent developments in the history of organizational governance.

Concentrating information is a mandatory process to retain a competitive corporate advantage. By producing e-metrics, an organization can improve productivity, the well-being of employees, and reduce operational costs as well. Technology enables corporations to improve the quantity and quality of information stored and accelerate the analysis and processing of this information. It also offers flexibility of information gathering in terms of supporting business operations.

However, it should be noted that there are many negative implications of this technology. For instance, in the past it was difficult to store billions of sensitive data, such as human fingerprints, and tracking and storing billions of fingerprints was impossible. Now everyone submits their fingerprints through personal devices voluntarily, in terms of personal identification services. Thus, today, corporations can exploit technologies, such as smartphones and tablets, that are capable of fingerprint scanning. This process has made available to corporations and technological companies a huge amount of data that can either be beneficial or spell the end of human privacy. Fingerprint scanners are already a 360-degree metric instrument, capable of tracking human behavior. For example, fingerprint sensors can be found under the doorknob, on the steering wheel of a car, on the back of gear paddles, or in public transport and locations where people are welcome. Also, in recent decades, many big cities have already deployed sets of street cameras, governing not only traffic but also human behavior. Therefore, many ethical concerns related to storing sensitive data are arising, because personal information such as fingerprints are among the terms and conditions of smartphone device manufacturers and gigantic international corporations.

In addition, global positioning systems (GPS) trackers are precisely recording the movements of individuals. Technology can provide companies with embedded applications for tracking human beings, making it possible to implant a microchip under the human skin that can unlock doors, enable devices such as printers, or run other programmable tasks. Insertable technology reflects the need of the business world to exploit as much data as possible. Corporations store, control, and analyze an unprecedented amount of digital data and information about individuals, and not only during worktime. Systems can record the amount of time people spend on leisure, at home, or on the road. They can track meetings and even have embedded technologies such as microphones to provide complete information on conversations. Also, technologies such as cookies are found on the Internet that can create a comprehensive profile of an individual, thus making it possible to tap into users' preferences on a variety of topics. A cookie is used for authenticating and tracking, as a mechanism that remembers the user's movements, such as webpage preferences. For instance, social media platforms use such technologies to promote their interests and provide their services to the users for free, as a reward for interacting with the platform.

In terms of corporate measures, e-metrics are not only about finding suitable training for employees, about supporting the recruitment process, or noting payroll and expenses. The functions that an electronic platform can perform are limited only by its user capabilities. Software suppliers can provide corporate systems that are customizable, based on organizational needs. Furthermore, many corporations use both external software suppliers and internal developers to create unique modified features that are more competitive and exclusive in the market. Upgrades are always necessary in this process of keeping a system up to date, and the use of advanced artificial intelligence, machine learning, and other information technology-related techniques of data analysis is mandatory.

It is essential to note that the use and maintenance of a corporate system must be done very carefully, as detailed enterprise schemes integrate all data and processes of an organization into a unified system with the same database. This demonstrates that a system failure could have disastrous consequences, and in most cases this cannot be reversed. This could explain why a corporation may sometimes prefer to invest more in technology than in other traditional organizational expenses such as wages.

Measures and metrics require a multidimensional system with multilevel analysis. Specifically, workforce composition data, such as sex, gender, age, race, health, employment terms, and contract length, can be analyzed to the extent of workforce characteristics and assess corporate needs in terms of employment contracts and specific terms. Skills analysis is also very valuable, as information systems can sort and filter results in the context of certain skills, qualifications, degrees, and educational background of human resources. Furthermore, the experience level and portfolios created from individuals' past employment relationships and outcomes can be a significant source of reference or comparison between individuals and candidates. Employee turnover rates and performance indicators can also be used in order to cope with shortfalls and issues such as number of vacancies as a percentage of total workforce, evaluate commitment level, compare actual with budgeted payroll and other costs, predict training needs and form development programs.

Each of the instruments mentioned must consider ethics as fundamental to creating a sustainable business environment, while the main mission of corporate policies must be the well-being of individuals. Metrics based on identification, authentication, or verification technologies are useful and practical. The expansion of the infrastructure of biometrics usage and capabilities indicates that corporate policies must develop methods of attracting individuals by providing 360-degree ethics. Technologies on information and data, such as biometric tools, must meet various requirements that governments and other regulators set for them. However, authorities develop practices about public technology and patents. This means they cannot pass rules on or control technologies that are at an experimental stage, undergoing testing processes by scientists and experts in the field, that have not yet been made available to the public.

Therefore, the ethical awareness of the creator of a technological innovation and implementation is critical. Policy makers must ensure security for technological adoption and exploitation of information. This is of crucial importance in regard to business ethics because conflicts arise between the interests of shareholders, the employees of a corporation, and the society in which the business operates. The *moral entity consideration* policy consists of an internal driving force to implement and develop ethical practices, as debates on the deployment and usage of data seem to be very difficult to reconcile in policy. Ethical standards and perspectives on such technologies can profoundly influence how data is exploited without harming other entities, and, thus, policy makers must take advantage of technological developments, while considering the interests of individuals that they affect.

It is worth noting that in the past, when the predictions for the widespread use of microchips were subject of intense criticism, everyone believed that technology will never reach the point at which it can be used against human privacy. However, although no one wanted to directly buy a microchip, everyone wanted to buy a mobile phone, making its adoption rate and usage even more critical for human health services. In particular, more households in developing countries own a mobile phone than have access to electricity or improved sanitation (The World Bank 2016). Furthermore, when consumers realized that they could not communicate without a mobile phone in their pockets, individuals became addicted to cell phones. Consequently, companies desiring to promote smartphones on the market found it easy to do so, because people kept buying these devices ignoring the serious threat to their personal data if the hardware and software providers could not meet their need for individual security and privacy.

Hence, is it wrong to adopt such technologies and exploit data analysis? No. E-metrics and biometric deployments can be extremely useful for both the corporation and employees, as well as for society in general. Problems are created when some individuals exploit technology over the rights of other people and entities. It is critical to create and develop sustainable legislative and operational infrastructure to enable rational technology usage, in the context of an international framework. At the same time, if regulation does not cover a technology yet, practitioners are responsible for its ethical exploitation. Data is used to make groups of individuals, to tag and categorize people according to a set of criteria, while advanced and intelligent systems record most of our routine. There-fore, practitioners must explore global practices and trends and consider ethical theories and implementations from multicultural concepts.

Confidential Ethical Systems

Ethical measurements and electronic information systems cannot ensure the universal development of confidential ethical systems. The morality of such mechanisms stems from human behavior. Hence, confidential-ity can be developed only through human actions in terms of informa-tion exploitation. Confidential conflicts emerge since information about something has limits on how and when it can be disclosed to a third-party system. You need to be an authorized individual in order to have access to confidential information. Therefore, corporate policies must include strong moral guidelines on how to cope with ethical dilemmas related to information sharing and how to decrease the volume of conflicts between the rights of different individuals, given a set of conditions and situations.

Corporations pose complex confidentiality issues. This happens due to the amount of information gathered, stored, and shared within the corporate environment and operations. Professionals and, in general, businesspeople, whether they belong to the top or bottom level, have a moral obligation to protect the confidentiality of information. This is everyone's fundamental moral duty and challenges the moral awareness of individuals. In particular, data confidentiality refers to the ability to share sensitive data among a community of users while respecting the privileges granted by the data owner to each member of the community, whereas data privacy means that the data owned by an individual will never be disclosed to anyone else; hence, because sharing is precluded by privacy, it is easier to enforce than confidentiality (Bouganim and Pucheral 2002). Therefore, practitioners and professionals who have access to databases also have access to private data and sensitive information. Corporate poli-cies must ensure that their access points on information will not work against the right to privacy, because the process of keeping private in-formation requires that the individuals involved be well informed about such practices.

Management of confidential information is not an easy task. Corporate fraud cases have been the main subject of criticism both inside and outside the business world, because it is believed that information along with money is more important and of greater worth than any other subject. Indeed, studies have found that executives who commit corporate fraud face greater financial incentives for doing so (Johnson, Ryan, and Tian 2009). However, what must happen to confidential information during legal proceedings or other circumstances such as criminal trials? Corporate policies must include a wide range of guidelines and avoid being accomplices to such conditions. Additionally, a global framework on such issues must be developed and updated. For instance, since the 1980s, practices suggest that U.S. law and practice concerning administrative and judicial disclosure of confidential business and governmental information in antidumping and countervailing duty cases would be ideal for adoption by the European Community (Taylor and Vermulst 1987). Thus, international law must cover a variety of cases, and corporate practices must adhere to the global law as well, where it fits.

There are a plethora of approaches that a policy maker can implement to conduct a comprehensive code of ethics on confidential information systems. Although there are some common principles, the standards governing corporate policies on confidential information and private data vary between entities. Some corporations have strict policies, and others implement more flexible schemes, given the continuous development of the field of information systems and privacy. Hence, even though the development of widely embraced ethical norms is a mandatory process, which all members of a corporation are required to adhere to, individuals tend to implement their own ethical standards on confidential information. Consequently, corporate policy makers must develop confidential guidelines as a matter of strong internal organizational policy, which no one is authorized to deviate from if the action is ruled by policy regulations.

Accordingly, if an individual discovers that his or her privacy has been breached, it is very difficult to develop trust and dignity among the same people. Leaked information can not only be painful in terms of personal psychology, pressure from public, and feelings that can change human behavior and perceptions, but it can also present legal consequences. If the principles of meritocracy, equality, and fairness in a corporation are under threat from information misuse, then, sooner or later, individuals could implement unethical practices to survive in an unsustainable environment. However, if the individual can afford the cost of leaving, then it is the only rational option, at least until the organization manages to implement another set of ethical principles.

Another great example of managing moral issues concerning confidential ethical systems is about genomic databases. In particular, the complexity of technology has required the rational management of information to be part of the workload of data scientists. This means that such progress and processing of data has enabled genotype analysis of individuals become a trend that it could be vital for the development of a series of corporations. A genotype is an individual's collection of genes, whereas the expression of the genotype constitutes the individual's observable traits, called the phenotype. The latter refers to traits such as blood type, height, or hair and eye color. The field of genomics generates data about the genome, as a set of genetic instructions found in a cell, and for a human it consists of 23 pairs of chromosomes. The short description of genomics presented is very important, as corporations could face a situation where biobank exploitation becomes inevitable. This implies that confidentiality about individual sensitive and private information is challenged, and it is critical to identify a clear relationship between different legal sources "where the impact of new technologies requires a coordinated approach to ethical and legal issues about informed consent, confidentiality, individual identity, discrimination, self-determination, the secondary use of samples and data, the return of results to the subject, and data sharing" (Mascalzoni 2015).

Thus, because human genomic data is uniquely identifiable, corporations may use them, and thus emerges ethical awareness. In particular, corporations may use such technologies of identification to ultimately control the access, sharing, and general management of sensitive data. Ethical issues emerge by the exponentially increasing volume and pace of genomic data collection in digital databases, because they can be converted into a coded electronic format for storage that is readable by every user. In some cases, you do not need to be a scientist or an individual with advanced biological knowledge in order to explore genomic databases, because the latter are expressed in such a way by data scientists and software applications that corporations and practitioners can use them for their interests easily. As statistical techniques improve alongside with the growth of databases, the association of genetic data with individual characteristics is a very powerful tool that corporations will be able to use in order to gain a competitive advantage and exploit their resources as efficiently as they can, to avoid any potential risks in information management.

Additionally, one of the most crucial ethical risks in data management is about the rules and procedures for allowing access to information. It is critical to set moral policies governing who should have access to that set of databases, under what conditions, and for what purpose, as already mentioned. For instance, if a corporation sells your private data as its client, in order to help a third entity to exploit your personal vulnerable dimensions, it raises critical ethical concerns. Imagine a company in the pharmaceutical industry that knows that most people in a specific town will have cardiac problems, due to special genetic conditions stemming from their biological ancestors in that area. This gives the corporation a huge competitive advantage, but at the same time it has followed unethical or even illegal practices in terms of data exploitation if people are not informed about the multidimensional use of their data, in accordance with the terms and conditions implemented by the corporation. Also, it is worth noting that the 2020 pandemic outbreak raised such concerns to a very high level, because the COVID-19 event occurred in a much more digitized and connected world where data quality and security controls are needed (Ienca and Vayena 2020).

Many organizations have been victims of their confidentiality policies. Technological giants such as companies in the social media industry or manufacturers of hardware have been found to implement such unethical practices. For instance, confidential issues include the leak of millions of e-mails and accounts from an e-mail provider and the leak or sale of private data such as demographic data, or even personal preferences on a variety of topics, or sensitive data such as personal text messages through applications and communication providers. In addition, a company may use data from its clients or business associates, in order to increase its competitiveness, or an organization may use unethical practices to reveal information that could be proved to work against the profitability and status of other corporations and competitors.

Apart from the foregoing, the leaked data can be used by external third-party entities or by individuals inside a corporation, as when an employee wants to learn something important about another individual, to gain an advantage such as a promotion, a bonus, or an achievement. Similarly, when a manager wants to promote someone, maybe from a personal preference and in order to cultivate a good interpersonal relationship with the individuals, even though there is another individual with greater attributes and contribution to the organizational performance. This practice of acting unethical and misusing confidential information is associated even with people with higher educational backgrounds and experience. A forgotten document on an office table could be enough to expose confidential information, and hence it is very difficult to avoid such circumstances entirely. Serving the best of personal interests could result in using confidential information against other people. Therefore, carefully thinking about the consequences is recommended before final action is taken, considering that interpersonal conflict may emerge from such activity.

Thus, people can control and prevent such inappropriate practices by paying more attention to the information systems and the moral awareness of their activity. Consequently, practitioners must minimize harm and approach ethical decision making systematically in order to protect the rights of individuals and develop an ethical, reasonable, and rational system on confidential information. It is essential to realize the moral issue; analyze what data, interests, values, and beliefs of individuals are likely to be affected; examine the benefits and risks of alternatives; and then implement the most suitable policy depending on conditions and variables of a situation.

It is not about the establishment of a general deontology that treats people as subject of principles and rules. Rather, corporate policies must inspire people to develop their own deontology in the context of personal and business ethics, their own sense of responsibility against other entities, regarding the consequences of their behavior, and whether they violate rules, rights, or law. It is important to implement strategies that prevent confidential leaks, even though in some cases confidential information is inevitable, due to the position of an individual, its weakness over ethical behavior, and the management of sensitive private data because of mandatory operations and business tasks.

Therefore, the existence of a code of ethics is crucial for business sustainability and the moral development of its employees. Categorizing behaviors into the ethically acceptable and the ethically unacceptable is a very demanding process, with many challenges, as explained in a previous chapter. In terms of confidential ethical systems, however, the implementation of the principles of a code of ethics is even more complex than in other common corporate operations. For instance, when an accountant realizes that a fraud case emerges considering specific corporate financial statements, or when an employee behaves unethically due to the relationship he or she developed with their manager, or when a company stores millions of electronic data with sensitive personal information such as online service platforms, data exploitation with the best of morals could be tough to achieve, though a mandatory process.

Concluding Remarks

Using advanced techniques such as machine learning and artificial intelligence that enable data scientists and professionals to harvest the available information in innovative ways is a compulsory corporate process in modern economics. Technological advances enable the management of information with multidimensional approaches, while emergent technologies can lead to many security and connectivity issues. Skewed data and technical limitations slow down human displacement in many business sectors; however, the owners or holders of information and technology as a combination of corporate excellence have a robust advantage against the competitors. Maximizing organizational performance through information management is essential for corporate success, as the effective analysis adds value to the decision- and policy-making process. Technology enables the use of an extensive 360-degree feedback mechanism for all corporate procedures. In terms of biometric technologies and their ethical implications, an individual can be used as a unique identifier. By using e-metrics, an organization can improve productivity and the well-being of employees and reduce operational costs. Additionally, insertable technology reflects the need of the business world to exploit as much data as possible, whereas corporations could be in a situation where biobank exploitation is inevitable. In any case, corporate policies must include a solid moral framework on how to cope with ethical dilemmas on information sharing and how to decrease the volume of conflicts between the rights of different individuals, given a set of conditions and situations. Corporate policy makers must develop confidential guidelines as a matter of strong internal organizational policy, from which no one is authorized to deviate.

CHAPTER 8

Ethics and Employment Relationship

Corporate policies are subject to the law governing business issues such as the level of minimum wages; maximum hours of work; standards of health and safety; and other rules in the context of hiring, promoting, and firing an employee. These corporate challenges are related to the general employment relationship, where a positive attitude toward a work climate of excellence and motivation is essential. Working in an inspiring corporate environment must be a mandatory initial strategic policy for each organization. The meaning of work is one of the most important aspects of employment. The time we dedicate to work is considerably long. It takes a major and vital part of our life, and thus we need to evaluate and prioritize work conditions, such as the importance of business ethics and other organizational issues such as operational flexibility. Factors affecting organizational and workforce behavior include the characteristics of people and the level of diversity, individual differences such as attitudes and personality, how individuals are motivated and engaged, and, generally, the organizational culture as a process that generates organizational commitment and trust among the involved members.

In particular, people can present differences in a variety of factors. Sex, gender, mental ability and intelligence, cognitive skills, educational background and experience, emotions, or culture and personality are only a few of the individual differences. People present divergent perceptions and reactions to change, morals and values, reasoning, memory, and verbal abilities, speed of learning and understanding, social skills, creativity and judgment level, critical thinking ability, vulnerability and positiveness in different conditions, straightforwardness, trust, commitment, engagement, openness and feelings, friendliness, self-discipline, recognition needs, and innovative ideas.

Additionally, globalized shifts in the financial, technological, environmental, societal, and cultural fields have a strong impact on corporate governance and on the expectations of the workforce and the society in which a corporation operates. Social dynamics and multidisciplinary issues have the potential to create conflicts and behavioral change. This calls for a positive employment relationship built on trust and mutual respect. Corporate policies must provide consistent procedures and practices, dealing with employee relations by applying fairness, meritocracy, and ethics. Emphasis should be placed on commitment enhancement, and general harmonization of terms and conditions for all individuals, by leveraging their capabilities and eliminating the weaknesses in their personality and knowledge.

Furthermore, the nature of work complements a variety of employment dimensions. Money is not the only aspect of an employment relationship, even though earning money is important for living, in the global money-oriented system of consumables. Rather, people work for further satisfactions, such as the opportunity to develop new skills and retain the existing ones, to be part of a greater team with valuable members, to do something important on both personal and societal levels, to achieve both individual and organizational goals, and achieve a status in life, as well as a multidimensional power based on work positions.

It is important to establish policies that enable recognition at various levels. First, individual satisfaction can be achieved through operational recognition, in terms of training deliverables and improvements in productivity. It is critical for a worker to be recognized, because it encourages him or her to contribute more, while increasing the levels of engagement and trust. It is important to note that there are differences between individuals in the mechanisms that drive job satisfaction and related concepts such as affective commitment (Hofmans, De Gieter, and Pepermans 2012). Also, the emotional impact of policies and behaviors is remarkable, because individuals usually expect to receive such recognition, by way of encouragement and appreciation. Even in cases where their contribution does not meet business standards, they would likely receive recognition by various methods, in order to encourage them to work toward success and development.

It is crucial not to force employees to sacrifice their perceptions or other factors that are valuable to them such as their free time. For instance, it is very risky to force people into social activities, when they simply do not want to, even though it would be nice and valuable to be part of such activities. It is not about the team as a democratic process of flattening everyone's beliefs. Rather, it is about the team as a place where everyone can contribute, where the individual can choose from among alternative practices and implement the method that is most desired and suited to his or her expectations.

Hence, undesired business environments can lead individuals to slow down and even get distracted easier. Given the fact that work is distasteful to some individuals who are money driven and status oriented, a fundamental policy among practitioners is to creatively supervise subordinates, make each individual feel useful and important for the corporation and society in general by sharing common passions and strategies, and form a business environment in which all members want to contribute to the limits of their own abilities and desires. In addition, this influential relationship between the corporation and its human workforce consists of a moral-ready and efficiently optimized environment of excellence. It is vital not to underestimate the impact of such practices on the relationship between corporate agents and employees, because cooperation requires a series of mutual concessions in the interest of developing a working atmosphere of appreciation and moral values.

Policy makers tend to accept ethical practices that they perceive to be relevant to their own principles. However, particularly in multicultural organizations, an individual represents only one side of the employment relationship. Various moral issues are perceived differently by different individuals, and thus everyone in a corporation must accept the thoughts of other entities, even if they do not agree with them. The logic that the one-size-fits-all approach is the ultimate method of managing such challenging work environments is unacceptable. Indeed, most researchers recognize that this approach is not the best solution (Davies and Schlitzer 2008). Although individuals could present some common characteristics and perceptions, this does not mean that they are identical. Thus, corporate policies as a set of ethical and legal measures that enable people to make the best use of their capabilities, realize their skills, and achieve satisfaction through their work, are critical for the implementation of a multidimensional and multicultural approach of satisfaction through the employment relationship.

The Moral Contract

Employment relations are emerging not just between an employee and an employer. Employee relations are affected in many dimensions, there being numerous parties with the potential to significantly influence corporate practices. For instance, the government plays multiple roles in forming corporate policies, as the ultimate instrument of legislating on employment rights and standards for both the public and the private sector. Furthermore, there are cross-national agreements, such as those within the European Union, or international agreements on common employment law between countries across the world. Also, trade unions and other forms of representatives, staff associations, and institutions are responsible for protecting and promoting the employee's interests, having been elected by their members to take actions such as exerting pressure on corporations to improve health and safety conditions as well as increase wage levels. Accordingly, leadership or management schemes are responsible for controlling and inspiring the workforce, through their decisions that have an impact on employee relations.

Moving on to a universal framework, the purpose of developing and implementing an employment law is to encourage job creation and make it possible and easier for individuals to be employed and to protect human resources from being exploited in the context of productivity without moral concerns. For instance, technological advancements and emerging financial conditions have created an international business trend and an environment in which there is no job security for many new employment relationships. This signifies that an individual will be employed if the corporation needs a human worker to add value to its operations for a certain period. However, this process of exploiting human workers on demand does not amount to long-term cooperation, which means that people cannot feel safe about their future, cannot make plans about their life, and cannot serve their personal interests rationally. Hence, it is critical for a practitioner to consider how individuals could be happier with the establishment of a moral contract, given that they react differently under identical circumstances. Practitioners must rely on cooperation rather than control and coercion in their relationship with employees. Consequently, the most important and fundamental principle is the *moral entity consideration*, that is, by putting yourself in the other individual's position and by trying to identify how you would react, what expectation you could have from yourself and the corporation under the same conditions, and what corporate policies could solve the challenge, while being legally aligned.

Employment law can be introduced at a local, regional, national, or international level, in response to political and economic transformations. New employment law and agreements can be introduced due to political actions or union campaigns or through individual initiatives. Regardless, the purpose is to develop a fair and ethical employment framework within which people can defend their rights, corporations can work by adding value and promoting good practice in the employment relationship instead of decreasing the value of its workforce and society, and, finally, governments can create an attractive business environment in which all parties involved are motivated and moral players.

Therefore, the employment contract must be aligned with a variety of agreements and standards, thus shaping a corporate strategy that can achieve consistency, fairness, and employee engagement. Corporations with high commitment systems have higher levels of productivity and lower levels of employee turnover than those with control strategies (Arthur 1994). Human resource control systems enforce employee compliance with rules and procedures, while commitment-based systems shape employee behaviors and attitudes by creating a moral culture of psychological links between organizational and employee goals. Furthermore, high-performance corporate practices influence employee turnover and productivity, the adoption of such practices being more important than ensuring that these policies are internally aligned with corporate strategy (Huselid 1995).

The capitalization of potential sources of profitability indicates that corporations will try to produce performance at any cost. At the same time, the production of sustainable efficiency consists of high-performance systems with high-value corporate principles. If people are negative and not interested in their jobs, then it is almost impossible to apply business ethics in the day-to-day procedures. Therefore, practitioners must create a strong and ethical employee relations climate, where consideration of other entities, trust, fairness, transparency, and willingness to cooperate lead individuals to moral behavior. Policy makers are largely responsible for the implementation and promotion of such practices in order to improve the conduct of employee relations and must therefore be well educated, moral thinkers, rationalists, trained in multidimensional approaches, and open to developing new theories and policies.

The moral contract represents that the individual is encouraged, motivated, growth oriented, and involved in corporate procedures in such a way as to ensure a balanced and harmonious relationship between the individual and the corporation, which, accordingly, encourages commitment and enhances productivity. Having the ultimate legal right to tell a worker what to do operationally does not justify actions aimed at exploiting the individual with unethical practices. The employment contract must be a comprehensive guide with legally acceptable notions that include moral standards, ethical expectations, and obligations, as well as the flexibility required to reflect the structural developments of external factors.

Paying employees their wages or salaries does not necessarily mean that an organization is ethical. Instead, it only signifies that the legal entity is fulfilling its legal obligations toward the employee, in the context of fixed terms in regard to compensation benefits and capital rewards. However, the employment relationship, or the moral contract, must cover a variety of other conditions as well. It must also be noted that there are expressed agreements and other types of contracts, such as psychological contracts, that may be conveyed orally or included in collective agreements and policies. In any case, when two or more parties agree on a contract, they must ensure its validity and consistency and develop mutual understanding of its terms, particularly its ethical dimensions (Table 8.1).

The dynamic relationship between parties in a corporation increases the difficulties of applying business ethics. The contract agreed between two or more parties is strongly influenced by corporate policies. Therefore, the moral contract is mostly an unwritten relationship, because individual behavior cannot be predefined and controlled by written agreements

Table 8.1   Moral employment contract essentials

Term	Ethical dimension
Parties involved	All parties to the contract must be informed of their overall rights, obligations, and other kinds of employment agreements.
Legal rights	People signed or involved with other kinds of reference in a contract must be offered the protection scheme of legal relations.
Contract terms	The terms agreed by the parties must be feasible, sufficiently certain, and morally acceptable. These terms include work conditions, work duties and job role, balance of work–life time, evaluation policies, supervisory forms, promotion opportunities, and contract termination rights.
Benefits	The contract must have a predefined reward package, in terms of the wage level, sick pay, and pension schemes. Also, it must include terms of additional allowances, such as reasonable health and safety benefits.

while it evolves over time. Thus, it is the individual's responsibility to behave as an ethical part of the business culture, whereas corporate policies must include comprehensive guidelines in terms of moral awareness. Consequently, a corporate policy maker must formulate procedures of moral transparency, approach the expectations of resourcing and developing programs, adopt decisions that do not affect other entities negatively, and treat the workforce as a valuable and crucial part of the business, relying on cooperation, trust, and commitment, rather than control, strict policies, and undesired actions.

Moral Corporate Culture

The establishment of ethical behavior must be accompanied by a moral corporate culture. The role of corporate culture in moral development is crucial, because corporate emphasis on profitability substitutes for the production of the desired ethical behavior through managing corporate culture (Reidenbach and Robin 1991). This means that people must have strong moral engagement and commitment to the corporation, two important elements affecting organizational development and performance. Retaining the workforce in a state in which the worker gives of his or her best, as well as remains proud of working, is critical for corporate sustainability. Therefore, developing the individual's moral quality is a process that is fundamental to excellence.

People working in an organization must be well engaged. This means that they should remain interested in their job roles and want to be as efficient as they can be so they can achieve both entrepreneurial and personal goals through ethical practices. The significance of people's engagement toward the employment relationship emphasizes the connection between corporate culture and workforce performance; in other words, an ethical climate affects organizational performance (Victor and Cullen 1988). In particular, financial choices of a company have consequences for the corporate culture (Guiso, Sapienza, and Zingales 2015), although it is important to note that some studies highlight the difficulty of defining the term "organizational culture," and the influence of subcultures has to be taken into account too (Lim 1995). Furthermore, an ethical culture can encompass both culture and climate. Organizational climate depends largely on the quality and stance of management and on the values to which it subscribes, whereas organizational culture has deeper roots in corporate identity (Collier and Esteban 2007). Indeed, there are a host of factors that have a great impact on engagement, such as work satisfaction, interesting challenges, room for employee contribution, responsibilities based on job roles and rewards correlated with achievements, the availability of knowledge development, the flexibility of work conditions, and the opportunity for personal growth through the corporation. It is also imperative to work in a high-performance and inspiring work environment that enhances employee efficiency and supports job needs with the required infrastructure.

Thus, there is a set of factors that can have a strong effect on business ethics policies and facilitates or complicates corporate strategies. "Ethical climates identify the normative systems that guide organizational decision making and the systemic responses to ethical dilemmas" (Victor and Cullen 1988, 122). However, developing a work environment that encourages moral engagement is difficult to define as a single procedure. Employment relations must be conducted within the framework of a general positive corporate attitude that leverages human resources in the best interests of both individuals and the corporate entity. Respect between employees, fair treatment of individuals, recognition of employee value and efforts, support for initiatives, and enhanced communication among them is the basis for cultivating a moral corporate culture in terms of people engagement.

Moreover, organizational commitment as a state of loyalty between different corporate parties has a direct relationship with business ethics. An individual must be inspired by moral awareness and a work climate of values and moral goals. If the individual cannot be satisfied by these mandatory ethical needs, then he or she will not be ready to exert any effort in the organization's behalf or desire to remain a valuable member of the corporation. Commitment proposes that the individual, instead of having to be controlled by strict rules and corporate policies, is sufficiently strongly committed to enhance and increase corporate values and performance, respectively.

Indeed, no one in a corporation, neither employees nor agents and shareholders, would want to be controlled by tight management, narrow vision, and strict responsibilities, because this could lead to an insufficient corporate culture, decreased organizational performance, and unhappy employees. Furthermore, it is vital to focus on how managers and practitioners frame an ethical decision in regard to a variety of moral issues that influence individuals' moral reasoning and decisions (Weber 1996). Hence, the morale of people working for a corporation is not only a critical factor in business success but also the key to corporate and individual growth. Commitment strategies must be applied with additional caution, aligning them with flexible policies. Following a *moral entity consideration* approach, policy makers can create value through people, influence their expectations, and make moral use of their capabilities.

However, corporate policies are affected by globalized trends and cultural developments. This indicates that even for a business based on local activity, there are some common challenges that have no borders. Thus, it must be noted that multicultural environments as multidimensional factors can potentially have a robust impact on a variety of business processes. For instance, human resource practice is becoming more and more challenging in the face of problems such as retention, dealing with culturally different people, and managing technological and informational changes (Vohra, et al. 2015). Hence, the spread of technological advancements can cause cultural homogeneity and value similarity within organizations (Fujimoto, et al. 2007), leading practitioners to adopt and use globally common practices by focusing on aligning people, processes, and systems to overcome such challenges (Morris, et al. 2009).

Thus, the challenge of employing a workforce with a sense of commitment is difficult to manage with a single policy and a set of limits. We cannot avoid change. Hence, to motivate people to work with commitment, corporate policies must include investment in training and development and increase cooperation consistency and trust, support participation, and employee contribution. The development of a sense of employee involvement creates the conditions for a moral work environment, because the individual whose feeling of belonging is enhanced, while being part of the business decision processes, will not accept being deceived.

Consequently, moral corporate culture relies on the development of ethical awareness, communication of common values and norms, acceptance of diversity in the context of contribution through different capabilities, cohesion, and the establishment of a fair and meritocracy-centered business culture. The latter can turn out to be dysfunctional in numerous ways: when individuals cannot communicate properly, leading to the discussion going nowhere; when team members cannot understand the corporate objectives and standards; when conflicts are quite frequent, particularly if they are related to personal characteristics; when the final decisions are made by some people rather than the whole team, so they dominate the latter and other perspectives; when there are strict policies that limit the use of multiple skills per procedure; and when there are no common values between the individuals and the corporation as an entity.

Given that people have their own values and norms, organizational culture consists of a multidimensional pattern of commonly acceptable and predefined behaviors and unwritten rules. In addition, it is important to mention that people can overcome their cultural needs, because they believe that this could be beneficial for their career, earnings, or their life itself. Individuals faced with difficult situations sometimes react in such a way that their values and norms can be modified in order to be aligned with the values and norms of others, because of circumstances and conditions that they might not be able to control by themselves. Thus, a healthy and moral corporate culture must secure the individual's perceptions and beliefs while developing a commonly held set of values and assumptions. But even corporations with solid values cannot be highly influential unless the individuals accept change and have aligned internal principles. Therefore, if the individuals do not behave in accordance with corporate ethics, they will be unable to implement business guidelines, and thus generate conflicts.

The association between individual perceptions and business norms is too complicated to be homogenized, as both factors initially present a negative intention to change, unless someone proves to them that the change will be in their best interests. Satisfaction and recognition are usually a priority in terms of persuading an individual to behave as you want, because he or she will feel a part of the system and a valuable part of the available resources. This suggests that their engagement, motivation, and contribution levels will be increased, as also the total efficiency and productivity in terms of business needs. Hence, the establishment of an enhanced business culture implies that there are shared values and a solid connection between corporate norms and behaviors. In contrast, a weak corporate culture evidences that values are limited to a few people, the employees have little knowledge about business ethics and policies, and there is little connection between shared values and individual behaviors.

Human resources cannot be treated like financial resources. An individual's professionalism depends on a variety of factors and skills. Individuals with advanced technical skills and abilities can have a comparative advantage over those who cannot cope with operational demands. However, behavioral attributes such as moral courage in the workplace are essential for developing a solid ethical character. In some cases, people tend to overlook the ethical aspects of an issue, in the name of financial performance and personal interests, or because their supervisors put pressure on them to implement such practices. This process can have a strong negative impact on the business climate, so employing individuals with moral courage means that they would be willing to adhere to the consequences of their actions and can influence other individuals to increase their moral awareness as well. Moral courage can be positively influenced by training in business ethics (May, Luth, and Schwoerer 2013), and thus corporate practices must integrate such approaches.

In conclusion, a moral corporate culture must be innovative, encourage creativity and change, accept risk-taking, even if it ends in partial failure, in terms of skill development and learning through mistakes, be fair and recognize contribution, build trust between members, be cohesive, and respect both corporate and personal perceptions, goals, expectations, and priorities. It is not possible to develop a corporate culture if it involves putting pressure on people to implement it as a set of behaviors in their operations. Business culture is about maturing through people, and, consequently, it is the individuals who are responsible for growing a sustainable and moral environment of rational behaviors. Involvement is highly desirable but also risks losing control over the implementation of corporate procedures.

Ethical Work Rights

Given both the creation of a moral corporate culture and the conclusion of a moral contract, the employment relationship is associated with moral rights and duties. This signifies that human resources have an extensive set of variables to consider, in order to make critical ethical decisions. There are legal rights, in terms of legislation and government regulations, and nonexplicit rights, such as issues in the context of business ethics. Each party involved in the operations of an organization can claim an assortment of rights. Employees, agents, executives, shareholders, government, and the society in which a business operates have rights, and they express them to each other when appropriate. This plethora of rights is limited only by an ethical standpoint and the *moral entity consideration* as a vital principle of human behavior. The various categories of entities can claim rights such as the right to receive safe and quality products and services for consumers, protection against the environment for a local community and society, rights in the form of legal and tax duties for government, and rights in the work environment and relationship for employees.

In view of this, the most vital right is that everyone has the right to be employed. The right to work is fundamental for our societies and for how they are constructed. For instance, if human resources were able to secure an income that provided a good living, who would still be at his or her current job? Who would be willing to work under a supervisor and an employer with strict policies and demands? Who would be at the disposal of larger corporations, in terms of creating value and delivering goods and services that need an industrial system of production? Also, given a society with an unlimited lifestyle, who would care about vital job roles such as rescuing people from accidents, including dangerous conditions of fire or floods? Would machines take advantage of their emergent intelligence and do these jobs instead of human resources, or would the latter suffer from greed and unlimited desires? Hence, the right to work is not merely a survival-based need, it is also a meaningful process of being valuable to society.

Most people cannot be satisfied with their job roles because various circumstances could not provide them with the desired conditions that could motivate their willingness to build engagement and commitment with their work. Matching jobs with available workers is a very challenging task for the human resources department, while practitioners must consider an extensive list of rights and duties from both involved parties in the context of a contract between the employer and the employee. Thus, the ethical work right in this process is to provide an equal opportunity to individuals to get employed, given their educational background and experience. This suggests that even the process of sharing a curriculum vitae with potential employers is a form of equal opportunity, because everyone is capable of sending an e-mail with his or her résumé to be considered.

However, because it is commonly acceptable, and even if it reflects some points of unethical behavior, some practitioners may end up making an offer to people they prefer. For instance, if you have two or more individuals identical in terms of their résumé, who would be the most suitable for the job? The answer depends usually on the process of a job interview or recommendations provided, whereas work rights begin at the point where the individual agrees to fulfill duties and do whatever is possible and ethically acceptable to achieve organizational goals within the context of corporate policies and demands.

Of course, not any job role is desirable, visionary, interesting, and meaningful to individuals. Indeed, corporate environments and roles that dehumanize people operate as a negative factor in motivation. Therefore, it is crucial to develop corporate policies that create the conditions required to protect and enhance work rights considering business ethics. Consequently, ethical work rights include a set of policies in the context of the right to a safe work environment, the right to compensation for injury and health issues, the right to engagement and participation, the right to job security and equal treatment without regard to discriminative factors, the right to privacy and respect for personal information, the right to be free from harassment and to have a say in such situations, and the right to have an explicit contract with respect to employee well-being.

The right of a healthy work environment is vital for individuals. Working in a healthy place is usually synonymous with the safety of employees. For instance, providing people with fresh air by installing controls to minimize airborne contaminants in a workplace and a smoke-free environment is a crucial practice. Moreover, healthy environments consist of a variety of additional factors, such as motivating people through positiveness and flexible procedures and by ensuring that they will not be harmed by others, in terms of not only injuries but also emotions and feelings related to work satisfaction, job burnout, stress, and risk-taking. Increased stress produces a negative impact on a variety of issues, including lack of control, time pressure and work overload, decreased productivity, creation of conflicts, lack of communication, and decreased levels of cooperation. Stress can be personal or even organizational, because a stressful work climate can lead individuals to inevitably be affected by corporate pressure and unpleasant practices. Additionally, workplace stress is a significant contributor to turn over (Schultz, et al. 2014), and thus corporate policy makers must be aware of such conditions.

It is important to note that in most cases a worker chooses to accept a job with such negative features, for a variety of external reasons, such as the need to survive, which leads the individual to accept everything at even minimum wages. This means that corporate policies must ensure that workers are provided with all the available information to enable them to decide whether they want to do the job, given that they have complete knowledge of the work conditions. Also, employees must have the right to some later choice, because new circumstances and conditions can change the work environment considerably. For instance, when there is financial turmoil or the company decides to exploit its human resources as much as possible under exhausting work conditions, or in a scenario where an epidemic breaks out followed by new employment conditions such as flexible blueprints for remote working, the worker must be able to evaluate the new environment and even leave the job without any contract clauses that could have a negative impact on the worker. Leaving a job due to changes in the worker's environment is his or her responsibility, but when corporate climate and conditions are changing, it is the responsibility of the organization in combination with governmental regulation. As a result, such vital information about significant changes in work environment should always be communicated to everyone involved.

Furthermore, employees have the right to job security. Corporate policies must be so developed as to exclude firing at will without reasoning. At the same time, promoting or disciplining must be aligned with corporate policies and business ethics as a rational process that prioritizes fairness and meritocracy. This does not suggest that agents and owners of a corporation cannot reduce their workforce. Instead, they are expected to accept and implement policies that protect the rights of both employer and employee, in view of the multidimensional character of the employment relationship, with a strong impact on both sides. Explaining decisions made by supervisors and executives and acceptance from employees if they are rational and understandable is a process of good and moral termination of a contract. Conversely, firing workers without prior notice or discriminating between workers or terminating a contract without considering its clauses such as compensation for leaving is an unethical practice that could run against the law and regulations.

Another critical right is about respecting privacy, because it is quite a demanding field of applied ethics. There is a clear difference between what an employee does during work and in the corporate environment and what the individual does with his or her personal life outside the boundaries of the corporation. Commonly, people cannot discriminate between the two, and they combine both work and personal life in a mixed and complex system of emotions, demands, and duties, making it vulnerable and quite challenging in terms of system sustainability. For instance, job burnout can be the consequence of personal life issues and vice versa, and individuals usually cannot understand and find ways of controlling their behaviors. This indicates that conflicts in personal life could be disastrous for the work climate, while the pressure of the work could similarly have a negative impact on the personal life of an individual.

Furthermore, it is commonly asked whether the personal life and individual choices should be under the evaluation process of practitioners in the context of corporate policies. Although it is very difficult to promote policies that control the personal life of a worker, this should not be the goal anyway for corporate policies. If there is something that the worker of a corporation should not do in his or her personal life and decisions, then it must be agreed on at the outset and analyzed with an extensive description in the context of a contract. For instance, a company could promote policies that restrict other employment relationships, such as working for a competitive company at the same time, in order to eliminate sharing of internal information that can be used against the company from third-party entities. Thus, corporate policies can include terms that could have an impact on the corporation itself as an entity and eliminate any other rules that could affect the personal life of the individual.

However, there are some situations that blur the relationship between a worker and a corporation in regard to what constitutes a personal issue and what does not. Thus, personal life decisions can trigger a series of consequences within the context of corporate policies and business ethics. Practitioners do not have the right to be universally informed about what goes on in an individual's private life if that person does not wish to disclose it, but they have the right to reveal behaviors and practices that could be unethical and illegal and that could have a negative impact on the corporate climate. Consequently, if an individual does something that is strictly and ultimately personal without consequences for other individuals and entities, then it could be called a personal life concern, or a part of privacy law. But if an individual does something that has a negative or positive impact on other people or entities, then it should be not only noted but also evaluated in the context of corporate policies.

An organization must not ignore the fact that its workforce has a personal life. However, some individuals share their job situations and incidents at work with others. Whether this is done intentionally or not, employees must be admonished to secure corporate information and personal work relations with colleagues and not share sensitive data about certain issues. For instance, if an individual uses the name of the company he or she works for or corporate data to proceed with unethical or illegal activities, it will have a negative impact on the corporation as well. Hence, an organization is not responsible for any harm that you do to others in your personal life, while corporate policies should promote behavioral guidance in terms of being rational and moral humans, considering the rights of other entities both during working hours and in personal life.

It is critical to understand your limits, and where your privacy ends, in order to clearly distinguish between corporate and private issues, based on mutual respect and moral behavior.

Furthermore, in the past a worker had absolutely no voice. Employees were unable to express their needs, thoughts, or even their problems concerning issues such as health and safety incidents. In most cases, they were afraid of being fired, because the employer had the ultimate power of ruling everything and everyone without any major feedback. Government regulations and law were not protective of workers, and human resources were usually merely a part of the production system. However, as the relationship between shareholders, agents, and workers changes, the latter is seen as a valuable part of the system, with additional meaning for the sustainability and development of a corporation. Therefore, policies for engagement and participation are crucial for a business, because without workers there cannot be a corporation and ownership in terms of an organization as a production system, and vice versa. In any case, it is suggested that both silence and voice are complex and multidimensional constructs (Dyne, Ang, and Botero 2003), in the light of passive versus proactive behavior, and within proactive, self-protective versus other-oriented activity.

This brings up the right to a living wage, as a fundamental need to survive. Here, it is important to mention some basic policies and regulation about wages. Most countries have a minimum wage level as a legal requirement to operate within public order and law. However, in some cases pay is not limited to work hours in terms of a given system, such as 8 hours per day. This means that the workday may be longer than the employee's scheduled shift and hours, due to additional time that an employee is required to spend on the employer's premises. Therefore, in some circumstances, the level of payment must be increased to match the number of work hours. For instance, given a standard of 40 hours of work per workweek, any additional hour must be treated as overtime, and employees must receive a fair overtime pay while being informed about the minimum and maximum number of working hours. Also, employees may voluntarily continue to work at the end of the shift to finish an important assigned task or to correct errors. This extended workday must also be paid, because the hours are part of work time and are compensable according to regulation.

Additionally, work time includes the period when an employee has been engaged to wait due to specific circumstances or the rest and meal periods. The latter are periods of short duration, such as less than 20 or 30 minutes, depending on corporate policies, and are customarily paid for as working time. Human resources need some time during the workday to regain some energy, be healthy, and, finally, improve their efficiency rates. For instance, a rest break after 4 to 6 consecutive hours' work is quite productive. At the same time, the employee is not relieved if he or she is required to perform any duties, whether active or inactive, while having a break such as for eating.

Moreover, it is essential to develop ethical policies regarding travel time. In the United States, the principles that apply in the determination of whether time spent in travel is compensable time depends on the kind of travel involved. For instance, an employee who travels from home before the regular workday and returns to his or her home at the end of the workday is considered to be engaged in ordinary home to work travel, which is not work time, while when an employee is given a special assignment in another workplace, the time spent in traveling to and returning from that place is work time. Similarly, in the European Union, when workers do not have a fixed or habitual place of work, time spent traveling each day between their homes and the premises of the first and last customers does constitute working time. Generally, according to the law and regulation, working time is any period during which an individual is working, is at the employer's disposal, and is carrying out his or her activities or duties.

Hence, providing human resources with a sustainable wage does not presume that the employer has the capability and authority to override the other rights, such as working conditions that respect his or her health, safety, and dignity, to be free from harassment, the right to equal treatment, or the right to participate in unions that have specific, rational, and moral demands. The purpose of ethical work rights is to develop a solid relationship between the parties involved and create a harmony among individuals to reach a balance point of excellence, which is the most suitable for everyone in a corporation. Although this is very difficult as it demands additional efforts and sacrifices from everyone, our moral responsibilities toward others as human beings must be strong enough to make this happen.

Concluding Remarks

Working in an inspiring corporate environment must be a mandatory initial strategic policy for each organization. Social dynamics and multidisciplinary issues have the capability to create conflicts and behavioral change. Therefore, corporate policies must provide consistent procedures and practices, dealing with employee relations issues by applying fairness, meritocracy, and ethics. It is critical for a worker to be recognized, as it encourages him or her to contribute more, while increasing the levels of engagement and trust. Additionally, cooperation requires a series of mutual concessions to develop a working atmosphere of appreciation and moral values. Moreover, it is vital to develop and implement an employment law, as an encouragement to job creation, and to protect human resources from being exploited. Practitioners must treat employees through reliance on cooperation rather than control and coercion. In view of this, policy makers must be well educated, moral thinkers, rationalists, trained in multidimensional approaches that they should apply, and open to developing new theories and policies. In any case, the significance of people engagement to the employment relationship emphasizes the connection between corporate culture and workforce performance. The morale of people is the key to corporate and individual growth, while the association between individual perceptions and business norms is too complicated to be homogenized. Business culture is maturing through people, and, consequently, it is the individuals who are responsible for developing a sustainable and moral environment of rational behaviors.

References

Alchian, A.A., and H. Demsetz. 1972. "Production, Information Costs, and Economic Organization." *The American Economic Review* 62, no. 5, pp. 777-95.

Arthur, J.B. 1994. "Effects of Human Resource Systems on Manufacturing Performance and Turnover." *Academy of Management Journal* 37, no. 3, pp. 670-87.

Auvinen, T.P, A.M. Lämsä, T. Sintonen, and T. Takala. 2013. "Leadership Manipulation and Ethics in Storytelling." *Journal of Business Ethics* 116, pp. 415-31.

Baan, R., Y. Grosse, B. Lauby-Secretan, F. El Ghissassi, V. Bouvard, L. Benbrahim-Tallaa, N. Guha, F. Islami, L. Galichet, and K. Straif. 2011. "Carcinogenicity of Radiofrequency Electromagnetic Fields." *The Lancet Oncology* 12, no. 7, pp. 624-6.

Babiak, K., and S. Trendafilova. 2011. "CSR and Environmental Responsibility: Motives and Pressures to Adopt Green Management Practices." *Corporate Social Responsibility and Environmental Management* 18, no. 1, pp. 11-24.

Bell, B.D, and J. Van Reenen. 2013. "Extreme Wage Inequality: Pay at the Very Top." *The American Economic Review* 103, no. 3, pp. 153-7.

Bewley, T.F. 1998. "Why Not Cut Pay?" *European Economic Review* 42, no. 3-5, pp. 459-90.

Blackler, F. 1995. "Knowledge, Knowledge Work and Organizations: An Overview and Interpretation." *Organization Studies* 16, no. 6, pp. 1021-46.

Bland, T.S, and S.S. Stalcup. 2001. "Managing Harassment." *Human Resource Management* 40, no. 1, pp. 51-61.

Bonn, I., and J. Fisher. 2005. "Corporate Governance and Business Ethics: Insights from the Strategic Planning Experience." *Corporate Governance and Business Ethics* 13, no. 6, pp. 730-8.

Borchert, D.M. 2006. *Encyclopedia of Philosophy.* 2nd ed. Vol. 9. Detroit, MI: Thomson Gale/Macmillan Reference USA.

Boudon, R. 1998. "Limitations of Rational Choice Theory." *American Journal of Sociology* 104, no. 3, pp. 817-28.

Bouganim, L., and P. Pucheral. 2002. "Chip-Secured Data Access: Confidential Data on Untrusted Servers." *28th VLDB Conference*. Hong Kong: VLDB.

Boxall, P. 1996. "The Strategic HRM Debate and the Resource-Based View of the Firm." *Human Resource Management Journal* 6, no. 3, pp. 59-75.

Brickley, J.A., C.W. Smith, and J.L. Zimmerman. 2000. "Business Ethics and Organizational Architecture." *SSRN Electronic Journal* 26, no. 9, pp. 1821-35.

Brummer, J. 1985. "Business Ethics: Micro and Macro." *Journal of Business Ethics* 4, pp. 81-91.

Burton, B.K, and M.G. Goldsby. 2009. "The Moral Floor: A Philosophical Examination of the Connection Between Ethics and Business." *Journal of Business Ethics* 91, pp. 145-54.

Buss, D.M, M. Gomes, D.S. Higgins, and K. Lauterbach. 1987. "Tactics of Manipulation." *Journal of Personality and Social Psychology* 52, no. 6, pp. 1219-29.

Cacioppe, R., N. Forster, and M. Fox. 2008. "A Survey of Managers' Perceptions of Corporate Ethics and Social Responsibility and Actions that may Affect Companies' Success." *Journal of Business Ethics* 82, pp. 681-700.

Camerer, C.F. 2014. "Behavioral Economics." *Current Biology* 24, no. 18, pp. 867-71.

Chapman, A.R. 2009. "Globalization, Human Rights, and the Social Determinants of Health." *Bioethics* 23, no. 2, pp. 97-111.

Clayton, J.A., and C. Tannenbaum. 2016. "Reporting Sex, Gender, or Both in Clinical Research?" *JAMA* 316, no. 18, pp. 1863-4.

Clement, R.W. 2006. "Just How Unethical is American Business?" *Business Horizons* 49, no. 4, pp. 313-27.

Collier, J., and R. Esteban. 2007. "Corporate Social Responsibility and Employee Commitment." *Business Ethics: A European Review* 16, no. 1, pp. 19-33.

Connelly, B.L., K.T. Haynes, L. Tihanyi, D.L. Gamache, and C.E. Devers. 2016. "Minding the Gap: Antecedents and Consequences of

Top Management-To-Worker Pay Dispersion." *Journal of Management* 42, no. 4, pp. 862-85.

Constantinescu, M., and M. Kaptein. 2015. "Mutually Enhancing Responsibility: A Theoretical Exploration of the Interaction Mechanisms Between Individual and Corporate Moral Responsibility." *Journal of Business Ethics* 129, pp. 325-39.

Davies, M., and B. Schlitzer. 2008. "The Impracticality of an International 'One Size Fits All' Corporate Governance Code of Best Practice." *Managerial Auditing Journal* 23, no. 6, pp. 532-44.

Demarest, M. 1997. "Understanding Knowledge Management." *Long Range Planning* 30, no. 3, pp. 374-84.

Dery, K., D. Grant, and S. Wiblen. 2009. "Human Resource Information Systems (HRIS): Replacing or Enhancing HRM." *15th World Congress of the International Industrial Relations Association.* Sydney: IIRA.

Deshpande, A. 2012. "Workplace Spirituality, Organizational Learning Capabilities and Mass Customization: An Integrated Framework." *International Journal of Business and Management* 7, no. 5, pp. 3-18.

Dyne, L.V., S. Ang, and I.C. Botero. 2003. "Conceptualizing Employee Silence and Employee Voice as Multidimensional Constructs." *Journal of Management Studies* 40, no. 6, pp. 1359-92.

Edwards, W. 1961. "Behavioral Decision Theory." *Annual Review of Psychology* 12, pp. 473-98.

Eisenhardt, K.M. 1989. "Agency Theory: An Assessment and Review." *Academy of Management Review* 14, no. 1, pp. 57-74.

Fan, Y. 2005. "Ethical Branding and Corporate Reputation." *Corporate Communications: An International Journal* 10, no. 4, pp. 341-50.

FCIC. 2011. *The Financial Crisis Inquiry Report: Final Report of the National Commission on the Causes of the Financial and Economic Crisis in the United States.* Inquiry Report, The Financial Crisis Inquiry Commission, Washington, DC: Featured Commission Publications.

Fong, E.A. 2010. "CEO Pay Fairness as a Predictor of Stakeholder Management." *Journal of Business Research* 63, no. 4, pp. 404-10.

French, P.A. 2015. "Corporate Moral Agency." In *Wiley Encyclopedia of Management*, Vol. 2, ed. by C.L. Cooper, New Jersey: John Wiley & Sons.

Friedman, M. 2007. "The Social Responsibility of Business Is to Increase Its Profits." In *Corporate Ethics and Corporate Governance*, ed. by W. Ch Zimmerli, M. Holzinger and K. Richter, pp. 173-8. Berlin, Heidelberg: Springer-Verlag.

Fritzsche, D.J. 1991. "A Model of Decision-Making Incorporating Ethical Values." *Journal of Business Ethics* 10, pp. 841-52.

Fujimoto, Y., N. Bahfen, J. Fermelis, and C.E. Härtel. 2007. "The Global Village: Online Cross-Cultural Communication and HRM." *Cross Cultural Management: An International Journal* 14, no. 1, pp. 7-22.

Glenn, S.S, and M.E. Malott. 2004. "Complexity and Selection: Implications for Organizational Change." *Behavior and Social Issues* 13, pp. 89-106.

Goleman, D. 2000. "Leadership That Gets Results." *Harvard Business Review* pp. 78-90.

Guest, D.E. 1987. "Human Resource Management and Industrial Relations." *Journal of Management Studies* 24, no. 5, pp. 503-21.

Guiso, L., P. Sapienza, and L. Zingales. 2015. "The Value of Corporate Culture." *Journal of Financial Economics* 117, no. 1, pp. 60-76.

Haldin-Herrgard, T. 2000. "Difficulties in Diffusion of Tacit Knowledge in Organizations." *Journal of Intellectual Capital* 1, no. 4, pp. 357-65.

Hargie, O., and D. Dickson. 2007. "Are Important Corporate Policies Understood by Employees? A Tracking Study of Organizational Information Flow." *Journal of Communication Management* 11, no. 1, pp. 9-28.

Hofmans, J., S. De Gieter, and R. Pepermans. 2012. "Individual Differences in the Relationship Between Satisfaction with Job Rewards and Job Satisfaction." *Journal of Vocational Behavior* 82, no. 1, pp. 1-9.

Hopkins, M. 2005. "Measurement of Corporate Social Responsibility." *International Journal of Management and Decision Making* 6, no. 3, pp. 213-31.

Huck, S., and G. Weizsäcker. 1999. "Risk, Complexity, and Deviations from Expected-Value Maximization: Results of a Lottery Choice Experiment." *Journal of Economic Psychology* 20, no. 6, pp. 699-715.

Huselid, M.A. 1995. "The Impact of Human Resource Management Practices on Turnover, Productivity, and Corporate Financial Performance." *Academy of Management Journal* 38, no. 3, 635-872.

Ienca, M., and E. Vayena. 2020. "On the Responsible Use of Digital Data to Tackle the COVID-19 Pandemic." *Nature Medicine* 26, pp. 463-4.

ISO. November 2010. "ISO 26000:2010 Guidance on Social Responsibility." *International Organization for Standardization.* www.iso.org/standard/42546.html, (accessed December 2019).

Jensen, M.C., and W.H. Meckling. 1976. "Theory of the Firm: Managerial Behavior, Agency Costs and Ownership Structure." *Journal of Financial Economics* 3, pp. 305-60.

Johnson, S.A., H.E. Ryan, and Y.S. Tian. 2009. "Managerial Incentives and Corporate Fraud: The Sources of Incentives Matter." *Review of Finance* 13, no. 1, pp. 115-45.

Jones, T.M. 1980. "Corporate Social Responsibility Revisited, Redefined." *California Management Review* 22, no. 2, pp. 59-67.

Jones, T.M. 1991. "Ethical Decision Making by Individuals in Organizations: An Issue-Contingent Model." *The Academy of Management Review* 16, no. 2, pp. 366-95.

Jones, T.M. 1995. "Instrumental Stakeholder Theory: A Synthesis of Ethics and Economics." *Academy of Management Review* 20, no. 2, pp. 404-37.

Kehoe, R.R., and C.J. Collins. 2008. "Exploration and Exploitation Business Strategies and the Contingent Fit of Alternative HR Systems." *Research in Personnel and Human Resources Management* 27, pp. 149-76.

Kelly, M., and A.L. White. 2009. "From Corporate Responsibility to Corporate Design: Rethinking the Purpose of the Corporation." *The Journal of Corporate Citizenship* 33, pp. 23-27.

Keynes, J.M. 2009. *Essays in Persuasion.* New York, NY: W. W. Norton & Company.

Knights, D., and M. O'Learyn. 2005. "Reflecting on Corporate Scandals: The Failure of Ethical Leadership." *Business Ethics: A European Review* 14, no. 4, pp. 359-66.

Kohnke, O. 2017. "It's Not Just About Technology: The People Side of Digitization." In *Shaping the Digital Enterprise: Trends and Use Cases in Digital Innovation and Transformation*, ed. by Gerhard Oswald and Michael Kleinemeier, pp. 69-91. Cham: Springer International Publishing.

Koveshnikov, A., H. Wechtler, and C. Dejoux. 2014. "Cross-Cultural Adjustment of Expatriates: The Role of Emotional Intelligence and Gender." *Journal of World Business* 49, no. 3, pp. 362-71.

Lado, A.A., and M.C. Wilson. 1994. "Human Resource Systems and Sustained Competitive Advantage: A Competency-Based Perspective." *Academy of Management Review* 19, no. 4, pp. 699-727.

Lawrence, P.R. 2010. *Driven to Lead: Good, Bad, and Misguided Leadership.* San Francisco, CA: Jossey-Bass.

Layard, R., and S. Glaister. 1994. "Introduction." In *Cost-Benefit Analysis*, ed. by Richard Layard and Stephen Glaister, pp. 1-56. Cambridge, UK: Cambridge University Press.

Lazar, S. 2017. "Deontological Decision Theory and Agent-Centered Options." *Ethics* 127, no. 3, pp. 579-609.

Lee, J.M. 1926. *Business Ethics: A Manual of Modern Morals.* New York, NY: The Ronald Press Company.

Lim, B. 1995. "Examining the Organizational Culture and Organizational Performance Link." *Leadership & Organization Development Journal* 16, no. 5, pp. 16-21.

Ludwig, D.C., and C.O. Longenecker. 1993. "The Bathsheba Syndrome: The Ethical Failure of Successful Leaders." *Journal of Business Ethics* 12, pp. 265-73.

Luetge, C. 2005. "Economic Ethics, Business Ethics and the Idea of Mutual Advantages." *Business Ethics: A European Review* 14, no. 2, pp. 108-18.

Lundy, O. 1994. "From Personnel Management to Strategic Human Resource Management." *International Journal of Human Resource Management* 5, no. 3, pp. 687-720.

Mantzaris, K., and B. Myloni. 2018. "Human Resources and Workplaces of Tomorrow." *International Conference on Business & Economics of the Hellenic Open University 2018 (ICBE HOU), May 11-12.* Athens: Hellenic Open University. http://icbe-hou.eap.gr/ocs4/index.php/ICBE-HOU_2017/ICBE-HOU_2018/paper/view/163, (accessed May 11, 2018).

Mantzaris, K., and B. Myloni. 2019. "What HR Professionals in Greece Believe About the Future of HRM." *International Conference on Business & Economics of the Hellenic Open University*

2019 (ICBE HOU), February 22-23. Athens: Hellenic Open University. http://icbe-hou.eap.gr/ocs2019/index.php/ICBE-HOU_2019/ICBE-HOU_2019/paper/view/40, (accessed February 22, 2019).

Marnet, O. 2005. "Behavior and Rationality in Corporate Governance." *Journal of Economic Issues* 39, no. 3, pp. 613-32.

Mascalzoni, D. 2015. *Ethics Law and Governance of Biobanking: A Very Complex Normative Puzzle.* Vol. 14, in *Ethics, Law and Governance of Biobanking: National, European and International Approaches,* by Deborah Mascalzoni, 1-14. Dordrecht, The Netherlands: Springer Netherlands.

Maslow, A.H. 1943. "A Theory of Human Motivation." *Psychological Review* 50, no. 4, pp. 370-96.

May, D.R, M.T. Luth, and C.E. Schwoerer. 2013. "The Influence of Business Ethics Education on Moral Efficacy, Moral Meaningfulness, and Moral Courage: A Quasi-experimental Study." *Journal of Business Ethics* 124, pp. 67-80.

McNutt, P.A., and C.A. Batho. 2005. "Code of Ethics and Employee Governance." *International Journal of Social Economics* 32, no. 8, pp. 656-66.

Miles, R.E., C.C. Snow, A.D. Meyer, and H.J. Coleman. 1978. "Organizational Strategy, Structure, and Process." *The Academy of Management Review* 3, no. 3, pp. 546-62.

Mohan, B., M.I. Norton, and R. Deshpande. 2015. "Paying Up for Fair Pay: Consumers Prefer Firms with Lower CEO-to-Worker Pay Ratios." *Harvard Business School Marketing Unit Working Paper No. 15-091*, pp. 1-44.

Moore, M.H. 2000. "Managing for Value: Organizational Strategy in For-Profit, Nonprofit, and Governmental Organizations." *Nonprofit and Voluntary Sector Quarterly* 29, no. 1, pp. 183-204.

Morris, D. 2004. "Defining a Moral Problem in Business Ethics." *Journal of Business Ethics* 49, pp. 347-57.

Morris, S.S., P.M. Wright, J. Trevor, P. Stiles, G.K. Stahl, S. Snell, J. Paauwe, and E. Farndale. 2009. "Global Challenges to Replicating HR: The Role of People, Processes, and Systems." *Human Resource Management* 48, no. 6, pp. 973-95.

Nerstad, C.G.L., A. Dysvik, B. Kuvaas, and R. Buch. 2018. "Negative and Positive Synergies: On Employee Development Practices, Motivational Climate, and Employee Outcomes." *Human Resource Management* 57, no. 5, pp. 1285-1302.

Noddings, N. 1994. "Conversation as Moral Education." *Journal of Moral Education* 23, no. 2, pp. 107-18.

Pedulla, D.S., and D. Pager. 2019. "Race and Networks in the Job Search Process." *American Sociological Review* 84, no. 6, pp. 1-30.

Persson, P. 2018. "Attention Manipulation and Information Overload." *Behavioural Public Policy* 2, no. 1, pp. 78-106.

Petit, P. 2007. "The Effects of Age and Family Constraints on Gender Hiring Discrimination: A Field Experiment in the French Financial Sector." *Labour Economics* 14, no. 3, pp. 371-91.

Pirson, M. 2017. *Humanistic Management: Protecting Dignity and Promoting Well-Being.* Cambridge, UK: Cambridge University Press.

Pirson, M., and J. Bachani. 2018. *Humanistic Management: Leadership and Trust, Volume I: Foundations, Cases, and Exercises.* New York, NY: Business Expert Press.

Pop, C. 2011. "Introduction to the Bodycom Technology." *Microchip*, pp. 1-23.

Porter, M.E., and M.R. Kramer. 2006. "Strategy and Society: The Link Between Competitive Advantage and Corporate Social Responsibility." *Harvard Business Review*, pp. 78-92.

Prewett-Livingston, A.J., H.S. Feild, J.G. Veres III, and P.M. Lewis. 1996. "Effects of Race on Interview Ratings in a Situational Panel Interview." *Journal of Applied Psychology* 81, no. 2, pp. 178-86.

Purcell, J. 1987. "Mapping Management Styles in Employee Relations." *Journal of Management Studies* 24, no. 5, pp. 533-48.

Ravitch, M.M. 1989. "Subjectivity in Decision Making: Common Problems and Limitations." *World Journal of Surgery* 13, no. 3, pp. 281-6.

Rees, C., K. Alfes, and M. Gatenby. 2013. "Employee Voice and Engagement: Connections and Consequences." *The International Journal of Human Resource Management* 24, no. 14, pp. 2780-98.

Reidenbach, R.E., and D.P. Robin. 1991. "A Conceptual Model of Corporate Moral Development." *Journal of Business Ethics* 10, pp. 273-84.

Renouard, C. 2011. "Corporate Social Responsibility, Utilitarianism, and the Capabilities Approach." *Journal of Business Ethics* 98, pp. 85-97.

Schultz, P.P., R.M. Ryan, C.P. Niemiec, N. Legate, and G.C. Williams. 2014. "Mindfulness, Work Climate, and Psychological Need Satisfaction in Employee Well-being." *Mindfulness* 6, pp. 971-85.

Schwartz, M. 2001. "The Nature of the Relationship between Corporate Codes of Ethics and Behaviour." *Journal of Business Ethics* 32, pp. 247-62.

Schwartz, M.S. 2002. "A Code of Ethics for Corporate Code of Ethics." *Journal of Business Ethics* 41, pp. 27-43.

Schwartz, M.S. 2005. "Universal Moral Values for Corporate Codes of Ethics." *Journal of Business Ethics* 59, pp. 27-44.

Sera, K. 1992. "Corporate Globalization: A New Trend." *The Executive* 6, no. 1, pp. 89-96.

Sims, R.L., and K.G. Kroeck. 1994. "The Influence of Ethical Fit on Employee Satisfaction, Commitment and Turnover." *Journal of Business Ethics* 13, pp. 939-47.

Smeltzer, L.R., and M.M. Jennings. 1998. "Why An International Code of Business Ethics Would Be Good for Business." *Journal of Business Ethics* 17, pp. 57-66.

Smith, M.E. 2002. "Success Rates for Different Types of Organizational Change." *Performance Improvement* 41, no. 1, pp. 26-33.

Stevens, B., and S. Buechler. 2013. "An Analysis of the Lehman Brothers Code of Ethics and the Role It Played in the Firm." *Journal of Leadership, Accountability and Ethics* 10, no. 1, pp. 43-57.

Strong, C. 2005. "The Ethics of Human Reproductive Cloning." *Reproductive BioMedicine Online* 10, no. 1, pp. 45-49.

Taylor, J.A., and E.A. Vermulst. 1987. "Disclosure of Confidential Information in Antidumping and Countervailing Duty Proceedings Under United States Law: A Framework for the European Communities." *The International Lawyer* 21, no. 1, pp. 43-70.

The World Bank. 2016. *Digital Dividends.* World Development Report. Washington, DC: International Bank for Reconstruction and Development/The World Bank.

Toor, S., and G. Ofori. 2008. "Leadership versus Management: How They Are Different, and Why." *Leadership and Management in Engineering* 8, pp. 61-71.

Trevino, L.K., and K.A. Nelson. 2014. *Managing Business Ethics: Straight Talk About How to Do It Right.* 6th ed. New York, NY: John Wiley & Sons Inc.

True, J.L., B.D. Jones, and F.R. Baumgartner. 2007. "Punctuated-Equilibrium Theory: Explaining Stability and Change in Public Policymaking." In *Theories of the Policy Process*, ed. by Paul Sabatier, pp. 155-87. Boulder, CO: Westview Press.

Unger, R.K., and M. Crawford. 1993. "Sex and Gender—The Troubled Relationship Between Terms and Concepts." *Psychological Science* 4, no. 2, pp. 122-4.

Verčič, A.T., and D.S. Ćorić. 2018. "The Relationship Between Reputation, Employer Branding and Corporate Social Responsibility." *Public Relations Review* 44, no. 4, pp. 444-52.

Victor, B., and J.B. Cullen. 1988. "The Organizational Bases of Ethical Work Climates." *Administrative Science Quarterly* 33, no. 1, pp. 101-25.

Vohra, A., A. Shrivastava, R. Premi, and S. David. 2015. "Impact of Information and Communication Technology in HRM." *International Journal of Computer Science and Information Technology Research* 3, no. 2, pp. 511-16.

Wall, E., L.M. Blaha, C.L. Paul, K. Cook, and A. Endert. 2018. "Four Perspectives on Human Bias in Visual Analytics." In *Cognitive Biases in Visualizations*, ed. by Emily Wall, Leslie M. Blaha, Celeste Lyn Paul, Kristin Cook, and Alex Endert, pp. 29-42. Cham: Springer Nature Switzerland.

Wang, P., and S.N. Yanushkevich. 2007. "Biometric Technologies and Applications." *25th IASTED International Multi-Conference Artificial Intelligence and Applications*, pp. 226-31. Innsbruck, Austria.

Wang, X.W., D. Nie, and B.L. Lu. 2014. "Emotional State Classification from EEG Data Using Machine Learning Approach." *Neurocomputing* 129, pp. 94-106.

Weber, J. 1996. "Influences upon Managerial Moral Decision Making: Nature of the Harm and Magnitude of Consequences." *Human Relations* 49, no. 1, pp. 1-22.

Westbrook, L., and A. Saperstein. 2015. "New Categories are not Enough: Rethinking the Measurement of Sex and Gender in Social Surveys." *Gender & Society* 29, no. 4, pp. 534-60.

Whetstone, T. 2001. "How Virtue Fits Within Business Ethics." *Journal of Business Ethics* 33, pp. 101-14.

Wolff, J. 1999. "Marx and Exploitation." *The Journal of Ethics* 3, pp. 105-20.

Zimerman, M., M. Nitsch, P. Giraux, C. Gerloff, L.G. Cohen, and F.C. Hummel. 2012. "Neuroenhancement of the Aging Brain: Restoring Skill Acquisition in Old Subjects." *American Neurological Association* 73, no. 1, pp. 10-15.

About the Author

Konstantinos Mantzaris was accepted as a doctoral (PhD) candidate at the University of Patras (Greece) at the Department of Business Administration with a doctoral dissertation on human resource management (HRM) at the age of 24. He was born in Patras (Greece) in 1992. He holds a master's degree in international business administration (IMBA) with a specialization in management with distinction from the Università degli Studi Guglielmo Marconi of Rome (Italy) and a degree in business administration (BA) from the University of Patras at the Department of Business Administration.

His scientific publications (papers) and research interests include HRM, business ethics, international business administration, leadership and management, policies, business strategy, and political economy. He has participated in international scientific conferences and academic seminars. He has significant experience in academia conducting university lectures in the field of HRM and labor relations, business strategy, and international business administration and as an academic seminar coordinator in the field of economics and management. Additionally, he has more than 500 publications of articles in media as author and contributor since 2010.

Index

OTHER TITLES IN OUR BUSINESS ETHICS AND CORPORATE CITIZENSHIP COLLECTION

David M. Wasieleski, *Editor*

- *Grappling With The Gray: An Ethical Handbook for Personal Success and Business Prosperity* by Yonason Goldson
- *Business and the Culture of Ethics* by Quentin Langley
- *Corporate Citizenship and Sustainability: Measuring Intangible, Fiscal, and Ethical Assets* by Jayaraman Rajah Iyer
- *Applied Humanism: How to Create More Effective and Ethical Businesses* by Jennifer Hancock
- *Powerful Performance: How to Be Influential, Ethical, and Successful in Business* by Mark Eyre
- *Ethics In The Legal Sector* by Carolyn Plump
- *Leadership Matters? Finding Voice, Connection and Meaning in the 21st Century* by Christopher Mabey and David Knights
- *Educating Business Professionals: The Call Beyond Competence and Expertise* by Lana S. Nino and Susan D. Gotsch
- *Adapting to Change: The Business of Climate Resilience* by Ann Goodman
- *Social Media Ethics Made Easy: How to Comply with FTC Guidelines* by Joseph W. Barnes
- *Business Ethics: A Moral Reasoning Framework* by Annabel Beerel
- *War Stories: Fighting, Competing, Imagining, Leading* by Leigh Hafrey
- *Leadership Ethics: Moral Power for Business Leaders* by Lindsay Thompson
- *Shaping the Future of Work: What Future Worker, Business, Government, and Education Leaders Need To Do For All To Prosper* by Thomas A. Kochan
- *Working Ethically in Finance: Clarifying Our Vocation* by Anthony Asher
- *Sales Ethics: How To Sell Effectively While Doing the Right Thing* by Alberto Aleo and Alice Alessandri

Concise and Applied Business Books

The Collection listed above is one of 30 business subject collections that Business Expert Press has grown to make BEP a premiere publisher of print and digital books. Our concise and applied books are for...

- Professionals and Practitioners
- Faculty who adopt our books for courses
- Librarians who know that BEP's Digital Libraries are a unique way to offer students ebooks to download, not restricted with any digital rights management
- Executive Training Course Leaders
- Business Seminar Organizers

Business Expert Press books are for anyone who needs to dig deeper on business ideas, goals, and solutions to everyday problems. Whether one print book, one ebook, or buying a digital library of 110 ebooks, we remain the affordable and smart way to be business smart. For more information, please visit **www.businessexpertpress.com**, or contact **sales@businessexpertpress.com**.

www.ingramcontent.com/pod-product-compliance
Lightning Source LLC
Chambersburg PA
CBHW061308220326
41599CB00026B/4793